52

MORE STORIES
FOR CHILDREN

R.E.O. WHITE

Pickering & Inglis
LONDON · GLASGOW

Contents

1 Our Holy Land

Lots of people seem to want to send me far, far away! Every year during January, the postman drops through our letter-box piles of letters, folders, and glossy booklets advertising holidays in all parts of the world, and urging me to join them. Some of the advertisers select especially Palestine, and tell me I *ought* to go there; and a few have even said I ought to lead a party in exploring the Holy Land. That is very odd, for I am sure that if I was in charge we would all find ourselves in Africa, or Australia, or Japan.

Still, it would be nice to visit Palestine, to see the places Jesus saw and walk the roads he walked, to paddle in the sea that Jesus preached beside and enter the little villages, climb the hills, explore the towns, and walk beside the river that Jesus knew so well. Sometimes we imagine we could feel him very near to us, if we could visit the places where he really lived.

Not long ago, in a little village in Yorkshire a minister felt like that. He longed to visit Galilee and explore Jerusalem, but he was rather poor. I do not know just why he had this strong desire, but his name was James Thomas *East* – so perhaps that had something to do with it. Anyhow, he made up his mind to save and save until he could afford the journey.

Ministers occasionally receive gifts from grateful people they have been able to help, conducting weddings or funerals, or advising them in great difficulties, encouraging them in serious trouble. Mr East decided to save up all the special gifts that came his way, year after year, until he had enough. And though it was not very long ago, he only needed about one hundred pounds.

The people in his church, and all his friends, were very pleased about the plan, for they were very fond of him. As the time drew near they made arrangements for someone to do his work while he was away, someone to care for his house, and attend to his letters and all the rest. And I have no doubt that the gifts were a little bigger, and came in a little more often, than usual.

When everything was ready, and the money-box was full, and some of his bags were packed, Mr East began to feel very excited. He sat in his house in the late evenings making lists of things to be done while he was away, and people to be visited and all the rest, but more often he just sat and dreamed of leaving the village, of the journey to the sea, and the voyage by ship, and then of first seeing the shores of the Holy Land. One evening as he was doing just that, there came a knock at the door.

Jumping up quickly, feeling just a little ashamed to be found wasting his time, Mr East opened the door. Outside stood a big man, with bulging shoulders and strong arms, but tears were running down his cheeks. Mr East immediately knew him for one of the men of the church and guessed what might be wrong.

'Whatever is the matter, John?' he asked, as he invited the man inside; the answer was as he had guessed. The man's wife had been ill for some time, and now the doctor had spoken very seriously to the husband. Only an operation could save her. But that meant she must be taken to a distant hospital, and John would have to stay near her; the operation would have to be paid for, and then would come a resting time near the seaside, if ever she was to be really well again.

'And you know, Mr East, that we cannot afford any of that,' said poor John, 'whatever am I to do?'

'How much would it all cost?' the minister asked.

'Every bit of a hundred pounds,' answered John – not thinking for the moment of anything else but his own sad fears.

Equally sadly, Mr East looked at John, then at his money-box, then at the bags packed just inside the door, and he heaved a deep sigh. The great dream faded, but Mr East did not hesitate any longer. Taking down his precious savings, he handed them to John, and offered prayer with him, and saw him to the door. Then, alone, he began to unpack his bags again.

I wish I knew if John's wife recovered, and had her holiday.

I think she must have done, for when Mr East thought it all over, he wrote a happy poem. He realised that we do not need to go to Galilee to be near to Jesus; if we do the things that Jesus would do, he is there beside us, wherever we are. In fact, when Mr East gave away his savings, he was nearer to Jesus *in heart* than anywhere else on earth.

How do I know Mr East had realised that? Well, read his beautiful little poem for yourself:

Wise men seeking Jesus
    Travelled from afar,
Guided on their journey
    By a beauteous star.

But if we desire him,
    He is close at hand;
For our native country
    Is our Holy Land.

Prayerful souls may find him
    By our quiet lakes,
Meet him on our hillsides
    When the morning breaks.

In our fertile cornfields
    While the sheaves are bound,
In our busy markets,
    Jesus may be found.

Fishermen talk with him
    By the great north sea,
As the first disciples
    Did in Galilee.

Every peaceful village
    In our land might be
Made by Jesus' presence
    Like sweet Bethany.

He is more than near us
    If we love him well;
For he seeketh ever
    In our hearts to dwell.*

(*J. T. East (1860–1937). Copyright: used by kind permission of the Division of Education and Youth, The Methodist Church, London)

2 The Industrious Blacksmith

Not all wealthy people show off, but some do. They seem to think that *having* good things makes them better than other people, whereas of course it is only *being* and *doing* good that makes people any good at all.

But a wealthy Frenchman years ago wanted very much to show off – to let all France know how successful he had been in business, how clever, and prosperous, and efficient, and all the rest. So he took his money to somewhere in the south, and built himself a beautiful house, in a great parkland of grass and trees, with a lake and quiet streams. The house itself was huge, a mansion, with many lovely rooms, high towers, wide stairways; much luxurious furniture, costly carpets and fine pictures filled the place. It made a splendid showpiece for a show-off full of pride!

Being the kind of man he was, he built a high stone wall around his park, to keep out ordinary people and keep his treasures for himself alone. Only at one place did the wall end, in a gate-house for the porter.

Then the silly man realised that while his own friends might come sometimes and see his wealth and comfort, no one else, living near or passing by, would guess how wonderful his house was, or know how much money he had made. So he enlarged the gateway, and put up a great stone arch, and made the porter's house big and imposing. And then he thought about the gates.

After much thinking, and looking at drawings of gates that he could buy, he was not satisfied. He wanted something more wonderful than anyone else could ever possess. So he sent to Paris for an artist to come and see his house and the landscape all around, and then design such gates as no one had ever seen.

The clever artist came, and walked about the fields and lanes, and through the parkland and the orchard; he watched

8

the birds fly past, and the fish in the streams, he gazed at the trees and lay in the deep grass doing nothing – until the rich man began to think the artist was making it a holiday!

But then the design was drawn, and it was lovely. For worked into the pattern of the gate was every wildflower that grew in the district, every fruit to be found within the local orchards, every bird and fish and butterfly and insect that the artist had noticed in his walks. When the gate was made, and its two halves hung upon their strong stone pillars, the effect was magnificent.

For once, the rich man was well satisfied. Villagers came from miles around to see the beautiful gates of his home: parties of townspeople from further off came in carriages to see them. It was said that when the evening light turned the sky to varying colours, the splendid gates appeared like fine lace curtains held up across the setting sun.

One day a somewhat shabby, dirty, untidy young man appeared and asked to be allowed inside the gates. The porter drove him roughly away. He came the next day, and was driven away again. The third time it happened, the porter told his master what was happening, and being curious who the young man was, the master agreed to see him.

The visitor explained he was a monk, who had walked the whole way from northern France because he had heard in Paris of the rich man's lovely gates. He said that he and his fellow monks were building a house of God, and he had come to ask permission to draw the gates, and take the drawing home and copy them, for their new church. But the rich man was angry, and swore that no one should have gates like his – not even God! And he drove the young man away.

For all that, three days later the young monk was back again, outside the gate, sitting on a box and doing nothing. The porter went out to send him away, but the young man simply sat, still doing nothing. He was there again the next day, and the next, and the next, and the next, just sitting doing nothing. So it went on for a year and a half: every morning, whatever the weather, the young monk came, and every afternoon he went away. The rich man saw him often when he went driving, but no one could prevent a man sitting on a box and doing nothing.

10

Then suddenly, he stopped coming, and was never seen there again.

More curious still, the master made enquiries in the villages round about. After some days, they found the house where the monk had lodged, and questioned the old lady with whom he had stayed. She explained everything.

Every morning, she said, her quiet lodger had left the house carrying his box: every afternoon he came home, and through the long evening he tapped, hammered, and blew his little bellows at a fire in the yard, shaping bits of iron on an anvil there. Gradually he had built up a whole pile of pieces, birds, leaves, flowers, fruits, fishes and butterflies, all beautifully made *from memory*. Then, she said, he hired an old donkey, and a still older cart, and set off to walk back again to northern France, with the pattern of the gate in his head.

I did hear (though I cannot be sure) that during fighting in the south of France, that lovely mansion was destroyed, the parkland became a battlefield, and the splendid gates were melted down for cannonballs. So the beautiful design was lost – except for the gates erected at the house of God away in the north, which the young monk had built up bit by bit from memory.

Bit by bit, line upon line, step by step, here a little there a little: first holding in your mind and heart something fine and splendid you have seen – then copying it yourself: there really is no other way for you and me to become like Jesus. Learning a little today, and a little more tomorrow, of what he said, and did, and how he acted, and what he suffered, not forgetting to 'go and do likewise'. It takes a lifetime to be Christlike!

3 Repeat Performance

Here is a very odd thing. Did History repeat itself?

I

Genesius was an actor, a very popular comedian, and exceptionally good at imitating other people. He drew great crowds to watch him in the days of the Roman Emperor Diocletian, something like 1700 years ago. But he is said to have become a Christian, in so very strange a way that when afterwards the church came to celebrate every year his brave death for Christ, the sign they used for him on banners and decorations was – the circus clown's cap and bells!

It happened this way. Before a vast audience, including the Emperor, Genesius was leading actor in a rather cruel play, which ridiculed and made fun of the Christians' way of life. He was supposed to be sick, and afraid to die, crying out in (pretended) panic for Christian baptism so that he might go to heaven. Another clown sat beside his bed, making rude remarks about God, and heaven, and baptism, and the Christians, which delighted the audience. Then two men, dressed like Christian priests, dragged in a tub of water and tumbled the sick man into it, with great splashing about and much laughter.

All this of course poured mockery on things that Christians held to be sacred, but people thought it funny at the time. Then, still in a sort of pantomime baptismal-service, two who pretended to be Roman soldiers came in to arrest Genesius as a Christian and bring him before the Emperor to be condemned to death: in that way he would die anyway, as a heathen, or because he was a Christian.

But suddenly, at the climax of the 'fun', and all unexpectedly, Genesius could not go through with it. Without warning, shame at what he was doing overcame him. He jumped

from his bed on to an altar to the goddess Venus, threw down
the statue, flung away his actor's mask, and cried out 'I have
always hated the name of Christian, but my family were
Christians, and now the truth has burned into my heart.
Never again will I make fun of the Christian faith . . . Here
and now I confess that Jesus is my Saviour . . .' He added
much more, that shows he understood well what he was
doing.

At first, the audience thought he still was playing his part,
and laughed at his show of earnestness. But soon his manner
quelled them, and they grew silent. The Emperor called him
over, and said very sternly, 'A joke can go too far: carry on
with the programme!' But Genesius protested that he meant
what he said, and the Emperor answered 'So do I' – and
ordered Genesius to be flogged.

So Genesius was beaten, and threatened, and warned of
death. But he replied, 'There is no king but him I now adore.
His I am, and shall be. I only regret that I knew him so late.'
Within a very short time – some say, only an hour – Genesius
was executed.

Surely that must be the shortest Christian life on record.
Indeed, the whole story is so strange, so striking, that some
wonder if it can possibly be true. Yet it is certain that the
church kept Genesius' martyr-day, on August 25th each year.

And there is something still more strange.

II

In a newspaper called *Life*, published by Christians called
'Assemblies of God', I read this story:

'It was the first night of a new play which had opened in
one of Moscow's leading theatres, a blasphemous comedy en-
titled 'Christ in a Dinner Jacket'. A packed house saw the first
act: a church altar arranged like a bar, with bottles of beer,
wine and vodka, fat priests raising their arms in drunken
toasts, nuns playing cards, and similar scornful ridicule of the
church.

The report goes on to say that Comrade Alexander Rostovzev, a Moscow matinee idol (or pop-star), walked on to the
stage pretending to be Jesus, and carrying a large New Testa-

ment. He was to read two verses from Christ's Sermon on the Mount, then suddenly change his manner, remove his Jewish robe, and cry out 'Away with all this, give me my dinner jacket and top hat!'

Rostovzev began to read, very slowly, 'Blessed are the poor in spirit, for theirs is the kingdom of God, Blessed are they that mourn, for they shall be comforted . . .' but then, instead of calling for the dinner jacket and hat, he stopped, as though paralysed. An uneasy silence gripped the audience when the smooth actor, his body shaking, started to read again, 'Blessed are the meek, for they shall inherit the earth. Blessed are they who hunger and thirst after righteousness, for they shall be filled. Blessed are the merciful, for they shall obtain mercy.' He finished the chapter, and the great theatre was stunned.

Other actors, thinking that Rostovzev was drunk, coughed loudly, called out, stamped their feet, urging the star performer to go on with his forgotten lines of blasphemy. But Rostovzev was no longer a blasphemer. Christ's own words had conquered and converted him. There, before the floodlights, he made the sign of the cross, and cried out in the prayer of the penitent thief on the cross beside Jesus, 'Lord, remember me when thou comest into thy kingdom.'

The reporter ends his story by saying that the stage curtain was lowered immediately, it was announced that Rostovzev was ill, and the rest of the performance was cancelled.

Is it the same story, 'translated' to a new land and a new time? Or did it happen twice? Two things we can be sure of: that the power of Jesus can change men in every age; and those whom he changes possess wonderful courage!

4 A Detective Story

Puzzle-stories are great fun, where you are given clues as you go along and you have to think out for yourself, before the story-teller betrays the secret, just what must have happened, and how, and why.

There was a young man, long ago, whose life and circumstances are wrapped in mystery. We really know nothing about him, except for one strange thing: he prayed an unexpected prayer. Nothing more than that! Well, that, and his name, which does not tell us much. His name was 'Jabez'.

This was Jabez' remarkable prayer: Jabez called on the God of Israel saying, 'O that thou wouldst bless me and enlarge my border, and that thy hand might be with me, and that thou wouldst keep me from harm, so that it might not hurt me!'

It's quite a little prayer, as some prayers go – on and on and on. 'Bless me and enlarge my border' sounds a bit odd: did he want to grow bigger, or fatter? No, it means that he had only a little place, a small home perhaps, or a tiny field, too little money, no real chance. One way or another he was poor, and he was asking God to help him prosper and do well. No harm in asking that: it all depends on how we get on, whether our 'getting on' is good or bad. It does sound just a little selfish, to ask this for oneself and not for anyone else. But if he was poor, with little opportunity to do well, we can understand why he was thinking mostly of his own need.

Besides, and here is another clue, his name does have a meaning. It means 'sorrow', trouble, pain. 'His mother called him Jabez, saying, Because I bare him in sorrow.' It sounds as though when he came into the family he was not very welcome, an unwanted baby! Perhaps there were enough already, for Jabez certainly had brothers, or perhaps they were too poor to welcome Jabez eagerly – just another mouth to find scarce food for!

His mother called him 'Sorrow' and she was sad: what

about his father? Did he like the name? Or was he even there? Had he died, or had he run away and left the mother and the children to look after themselves? We are getting on, aren't we! Jabez was poor, his home was poor, his mother apparently alone, with other brothers to care for too. 'O that thou wouldst bless me, and enlarge my borders . . .'

And here is another clue. Jabez asks God, 'O that thou wouldst keep me from harm, so that it might not hurt me!' Jabez was afraid – but afraid of what? He says, 'harm', something that might 'hurt' him. And he wanted God's hand with him, to keep him from it. We cannot be absolutely sure, but in Jabez' own language the words used meant *evil* things, wrong, bad, things; not just things that hurt like accidents, and toothache, and being ill, but lying, dishonesty, being spiteful, stealing, being sinful. That is why Jabez wants God's hand to keep *him* from *it* – from temptation and from doing wrong.

What does that tell us? That Jabez felt weak, and sorely tempted, and afraid that without God he would go badly astray, and fall into wicked ways. Perhaps not having a father to help him, and be his friend and adviser, made Jabez feel like that. Or perhaps because he was so poor, he felt tempted to steal, or be dishonest. We only know that he knew his danger, and he prayed about it. That was very wise.

Are we imagining too much about Jabez? Well, listen to this: 'Jabez was more honourable than his brothers.' Now that's a clue, if you like. Here now is a family that has been getting into trouble: the older brothers are well known not to be 'honourable' young men. No wonder their mother was sad, with no money, no husband, and boys whom no one trusted, or liked, or looked up to. And no wonder that young Jabez felt afraid that he might become like his brothers, a dishonourable man. Their bad example could lead him astray; they could persuade him into wrong, if he did not stand firm. 'O that thy hand might be with me, and that thou wouldst keep me from harm, so that it might not hurt me!'

Hearing that about Jabez' brothers makes us wonder again what sort of man his father was, and we notice two more strange things which may be clues. We do not even know his father's name, nor the village, or the city, that he came from. That is very unusual, for in Israel your father's name was always important, and a boy was usually known as 'So-and-so, *son of* So-and-so'. If your name was a common one, then most often the place you came from was added too, like 'David, the son of Jesse, of Bethlehem Ephratah'. But poor Jabez appears in the Bible without a father's name or a native place. That, and the brothers being dishonourable, makes us wonder if the father, too, had been in some disgrace. Was he too a dishonourable man, so that his name and birthplace were deliberately forgotten? Is that how the father disappeared, and the family's fortunes sank so low, and the brothers grew up in evil ways? No wonder Jabez felt lonely and afraid, and prayed that God would deliver him from evil.

What else can we find out about Jabez? Oh yes, the Bible says 'God granted his request'. We might have guessed that, perhaps, since the little story was preserved, and evidently known in Israel. If he had not done well, no one would have remembered him or written down his prayer. Besides, that tribute paid to him – that he turned out more honourable than his brothers, shows that people thought him the fine exception in his family. Plainly, then, God heard his prayer, granted his request, set his hand upon him and kept him from evil. Did God 'enlarge his borders' too?

I think so. For not far from this story, though in quite a different connection, the Bible says that 'the families also of the scribes that dwelt at Jabez' were descendants of Hur. That really is fascinating: it looks as if, although no one knew where his father came from, people did come to know where Jabez belonged, that there was a village named after him, some tiny place where he had prospered, and bought land, and raised his family, and lived his life honourably and well. And so the place came to be called 'Jabez' place', and then of course just 'Jabez'.

One other point is interesting too. This came to be the place where *scribes* lived. They were the writers who copied out God's law, taught it to the people, and to the children, and advised people how to live so as to please God.

Isn't that rather wonderful? Jabez himself grew up poor and in trouble, with no father to teach or help him, with brothers who were bad, his mother so brokenhearted that she called her new baby 'Sorrow'. And Jabez himself felt weak, lonely, and sorely tempted to go wrong ways. Yet afterwards, remembering all that, and wanting other young people to have a better chance and better teaching, Jabez' home and village becomes a place famous for teachers and for students, and for the knowledge of God's word.

And all because Jabez, in his trouble, prayed that God would bless him, and deliver him from evil.

In the Lord's Prayer, Jesus taught us all to pray that, every day.

5 Watch Your Feet!

> A centipede was happy quite
> Until a frog, in fun,
> Said, 'Pray, which leg comes after which?' –
> It lay distracted in a ditch
> Considering how to run!

Most of us manage to walk without thinking much about it. We do not need continually to watch our feet, except perhaps in snowy weather. On the whole it is better to look where you are going.

But feet can tell us a lot of things, for all that. Footprints were studied long before fingerprints, and expert trackers could tell from very faint footmarks who had passed that way, and how long ago, and whether they were walking or running, man or woman – and sometimes, even whether they were carrying anything! It had to do with the depth of the footmark, whether the toe or the heel made the deeper imprint, how far apart the footmarks were, and so on: it was all written there in the footprints, for those clever enough to read.

Mr Sherlock Holmes, detective, could tell much from the shoes a man was wearing, or had worn. Those of a city gentleman who stood behind a counter all day would look very different from those of a man who spent his day walking from house to house. A man living in a town, and walking smooth pavements, who for all that liked thick leather soles and high sides to his boots, was almost certainly one who had belonged originally to the countryside and deep muddy lanes, before moving into town. Any soil or dust in the creases of the leather could tell Mr Holmes where the man had been!

Long ago a man would buy or sell a piece of land by throwing his shoe across it: presumably, the buyer could produce the shoe as a sort of receipt to prove the land was his. And the Bible contains one of the most charming love stories of the world, which ends in a marriage announced to everybody by the happy husband giving the same kind of receipt for his bride – one of his shoes! We still occasionally see an old boot tied behind a wedding-car, to bring the happy couple 'luck' – whatever that means.

Fairytales, too, are full of stories of dancing shoes that will not stop until the unhappy wearer drops exhausted; of seven-league-boots that enable captives to escape or heroes to catch evil men, with mile-long strides; of glass slippers that show who is the true lady for Prince Charming. Glass slippers do not sound very comfortable, all the same.

In ancient Greece Apelles was a famous painter, and friend of Alexander the Great. Not unnaturally, he was a proud man, who hated any criticism of his work, and despised those who thought they could paint better. One of his tricks was to exhibit outside his house an unfinished painting, and then in disguise mingle with the passers-by, laughing quietly at their ignorant comments. Then, when the picture was finished, he would show it again, to prove how foolish all the critics had been.

But one day he overheard a rough-looking workman explaining at great length to a number of his neighbours how hopelessly wrong one painting was. One by one he listed the mistakes the painter had made – no human foot could be turned at the angle the painter had shown it; no shoe could be tied in the way the painter pretended; the muscles of the painted leg were all out of place; the foot was a shade too big – and so on. Angrily pushing through the group around the picture, Apelles demanded to be told how the workman dared to pretend that he knew better how feet and shoes should look. 'Sir,' the man answered proudly, 'I am a maker of shoes.' There was no more to be said.

Exploring Glasgow's ancient cathedral one day I was reminded of Apelles and the cobbler who understood about feet. For in the beautiful old choir-room, with its fine stone floor and pillars and old oak doors, there are worn places where for hundreds of years the choir boys left their outdoor shoes when they formed their procession for worship, wearing softer slippers for the sanctuary.

And inlaid in the stones of the ancient floor are simple reminders to the boys of the need to watch where they put their feet –

'Ponder the paths of thy feet, that thy ways may be established.'

'He that walketh uprightly walketh surely.'

'Hold up my going in thy paths, that my footsteps slip not.'

'Run with patience the race that is set before us.'

Christ came 'to guide our feet into the way of peace'.

Whoever planned that knew boys about as well as he knew his Bible!

Mind how *you* go.

6 The Empty House

I remembered this story while we were busy moving house.

Have you ever had to do that – to move everything you have from one house to another, and learn to live in a new place? It is exciting, but exhausting too. There is so much work to do, but it is fun to explore a 'new' house, one that is new to you if not to anyone else.

All the switches seem to be in the wrong place: you reach for them where they used to be, but now they are higher up, or on the other side of the door. The door handles are on the other side too. It takes quite a long time to remember that there is one more step now in the stairs – your feet will keep forgetting. For some days I had to try two or three doors before I could find the bathroom, and our poor cat was equally puzzled. All her favourite hiding-places had disappeared; she did not much like this new home, and she showed it.

We even lost the cat for a while. Some workmen opened up the floor to do something to the gas pipes, and then went away for lunch. When they came back they finished the work, replaced the floor, and went home. We did not see Sian for nearly three days, and then we had to open up the floor again. She crept out looking very annoyed, and sorry for herself at the same time.

Of course you think you are moving into an empty house, but you quickly find it is not really empty. Walking through the new rooms, that without furniture seemed so big and echoed to our steps, we found a wasp – in January! – and a bumble bee that had crept into a warm corner for the winter, and a very tiny but very pretty spider. Nothing stays empty very long.

That is what recalled the story, which I heard or read (I forget which) long ago. An old man lived in a house on a hill, an unhappy, unfriendly, surly old man, who would let no one visit him, or enter his house at all. He kept the door shut, and the world at bay. There he lived alone, and there he died, still alone; and the house soon fell into decay.

After a while people said that something must be done about the old man's house. Either it must be put in order and let to some new tenant, or it must be pulled down. It was not safe to leave it empty.

But when the workmen came from the Council to see what was to be done, they found the house was not empty at all. First the wind had got in, and had blown some slates from the roof, and whistled gaily through the dull and dusty rooms. That had let some bats get in, who lived among the rafters and multiplied their families. The wind had also shaken loose a window, until a pane had broken, and in came a butterfly, and at night some moths. An inquisitive bee made its way in and buzzed cheerily against the window glass, unable to find the way out. Innumerable flies, as usual, appeared from nowhere and seemed to live on nothing.

Now that there was no one to drive them away, a few birds, greatly daring, had nested under the gutters beneath the roof. During one storm, the wind had rushed through the holes so fiercely that the back door had rattled off its latch and hung partly open: full of curiosity, a few rabbits had come to explore this new burrow, and they had had family after family. The field-mice can get in anywhere, and so can spiders: nothing stays empty very long.

If I remember rightly, when the workmen counted up, not bothering about the flies and the bee, the spiders and the butterflies, there were *forty-three* tenants living happily in the 'empty' house. Wouldn't the old man have been furious, had he known!

Nothing stays empty very long: as your clever older brother or sister might put it, 'Nature abhors a vacuum' – it means the same thing. A tin left carelessly in the hedge by picnickers soon has a spider or a grub curled up snugly inside; a bottle lying on the beach quickly becomes a home, or at least a shelter, for some small creature. Jesus, you remember, said something like this once.

He told of a house that had been swept and decorated, painted and repaired, everything made neat and trim, and then left empty. And how very soon all kinds of evil things gathered together and broke in and took possession and lived there wildly, without care for anything. As a result, he said, the last state of that house was worse than before it was repaired and decorated. And all because it had been left empty.

What did Jesus mean? That it is never enough to try to put right the wrong things in our lives by just clearing out what is bad. It is never enough to say – only – 'I will not be ill-tempered', 'I will not be dishonest – or impure – or selfish' and think that *that* will put everything right. That only leaves our minds, our hearts, our time, empty and unoccupied – and nothing stays empty very long. We have to let in good things, like love and joy and truth and kindness and care for others, to take possession and keep out the bad.

When you think about it, is that not why Jesus promised that after he had gone, his Spirit would come and live within the minds and hearts of his disciples? An empty life attracts all kinds of evil –

Come into my heart, Lord Jesus:
There is room in my heart for Thee!

7 A Real Princess

Yes, she was real, though she lived so long ago, in fact about sixteen hundred years ago. And she was a Princess, twice over. I mean that through her father she belonged to the ancient family, the Julians of Rome, who traced their line back to Romulus and Remus, who were supposed to have founded the city and the Empire. That is why her name was Julia, and how proud she must have been of it! On the other hand, at the same time she belonged through her mother to the equally ancient and famous family of Agamemnon, King of the Greeks.

You cannot be more of a Princess than that!

And she had plenty to make her proud, as she listened to the stories told over and over again of what her great ancestors had done for Greece and for Rome. Besides, she was very rich. And well educated too, for she was able to read in several languages. She loved music, and possessed a good voice which she well knew how to use. So, though her father had died while she was still young, Julia lived happily with her mother, the Lady Paula, and enjoyed being a Princess.

Julia was full of life. She had a very odd nickname, we are told: 'Julia good-shot'. It is supposed to mean that she was quick-thinking, bright, intelligent, 'always on the ball' as we would say. But I wonder if it really meant 'good sport', meaning a reasonably well-behaved tomboy, full of spirit and of fun, perhaps of mischief too. For she had a brother: and brothers and sisters do get into mischief sometimes.

Both Julia and her mother were eager Christians, and everything we know about them comes from letters written to them by a famous Christian leader called Jerome. Now Jerome at that time taught and wrote at Bethlehem – that's right, *Bethlehem* – and a day came when the Lady Paula and the Princess Julia decided to join Jerome at Bethlehem and help him with his work.

So the lovely house and the proud estate were left behind, and there at Bethlehem they built a huge monastery, using the great family fortune, and began to gather students, men and women, from other noble families and from ordinary ones to train them for Christ's work. Jerome was the principal teacher: Paula and Julia, helped by many others, organised the work and cared for the students.

At Bethlehem, all the workers lived together, sharing equally the life, the food, the ordinary duties: none was proud, or privileged. In one letter Jerome describes Julia at that time: the scriptures 'bubbling up from her heart'; entering into fasting and prayer for the sheer joy of showing her love for Christ; and training her companions in singing – a *girls'* choir for Christ was something rare in those days. Other girls she taught to play the lute, an orchestra for the Saviour: or, as we would say, she created a Gospel Group, with vocalists and strings, and made a real hit. Jerome adds admiringly that Julia could sing the Psalms in Hebrew far better than he could himself.

But there was more to do than studying and singing. Very many poor people lived around Bethlehem, with crowds of needy and unwanted children. So Julia and her helpers provided food, cooking and distributing it themselves, and sewed clothes and took them round, and gathered the children into shelters to be cared for. When Paula died, Jerome had to write to Julia, for he was away, and tell her that – out of all that money – 'Your mother has not left you a penny piece, only a mass of debts, and crowds of needy boys and girls to go on helping.' But he added, 'that, after all, is a splendid inheritance.'

We might not think so, but Julia would agree. She added to all the rest that she was doing a guest house for Christian tourists on pilgrimage to the Holy Land. But bad times were coming, with war, and invasion, by peoples who did not know the Christian way. Hosts of refugees fled before them, crowding into Palestine and other eastern lands, homeless and penniless. Many of these sought help and shelter at Julia's monastery in Bethlehem.

It was at that time Jerome wrote to Julia's brother in Rome something well worth remembering. He recalled the days when Julia had come to Bethlehem, rich and ladylike, a Princess indeed, and he adds: 'I was not there in those days, but they tell me she used to be too dainty to walk in muddy streets, and had servants to carry her; she used to find even silk clothes too heavy for her, and the sun always too hot, but now, soiled and sober in her dress, she trims lamps, sweeps floors, cleans vegetables, puts cabbage in the pot, lays tables, passes cups and plates, runs to and fro waiting on others . . . If Joseph and Mary came now to Bethlehem, they would find shelter and a welcome.'

Isn't that wonderful? For to give food and clothes and shelter to unloved children, and the homeless and the poor, was to give welcome to Jesus himself. Jesus said so.

A really *Christian* Princess.

8 Leave Me Alone!

Everyone loves the story of Peter, who followed Jesus so eagerly, who spoke so often out of turn, saying the wrong thing, 'putting his foot in it'; who boasted rather too much about his loyalty to Jesus and yet when danger threatened denied three times that he was a disciple. We all like the promise that Jesus made at the beginning to Peter: 'You are Simon, you shall be Peter, which means a rock'; and the way that Jesus at the end led Peter to retrace his disloyal steps by asking him three times, 'Do you love me?'

All this we know, and like. But there is one thing that puzzles us. That is Peter's strange outburst after the miracle beside the lake.

Jesus had borrowed Peter's boat for a pulpit, and had preached from the prow to the crowd across the water. Then Jesus suggested that Peter launch out into deeper water and let down his net for fish. Although they had failed to catch anything all night, they now caught so many that the net broke, and they filled two ships. Then came Peter's astonishing reaction – 'Leave me alone, Lord, for I am a sinful man.'

We can only guess at the reasons for that odd prayer. The likeliest seems to be that Peter had been trying hard to follow Christ's ways, since they had first met and he had received that promise of a new name. But old habits, like swearing and bad temper, die hard, and Peter felt that he had failed, that it was no use trying to be a disciple. Now Jesus has come again and shown Peter how to do better the one thing Peter thought he could do so well – the Carpenter teaching the fisherman how to fish!

By himself, Peter failed, even at fishing: with Jesus in charge, Peter can do anything. Peter saw the meaning in Christ's action, but he still felt he would never make it. 'Leave me alone, Lord; find someone better; I am a sinful, wicked failure; just let me be.' But Jesus would not give up. 'Come,' he said, 'I will show you how to catch much bigger fish than these. I will make you a fisher of men.'

I first felt that I knew how Peter felt, and why Jesus so replied, when I read a famous London minister's story of two people who came to him in his church room after morning service, for a private talk. One was a young girl who only six weeks before had reached her decision to follow Christ, and had joined the church with high hope of a happy and useful Christian life. Now she came back to the minister in a mood very like Peter's. 'It's no good,' she said, 'I cannot go on. I am giving up Christianity, because it does not work.'

Almost in tears, the girl went on to explain that she had a fierce temper, which she had tried again and again to master, often praying about it, always sorry when she let herself go, but with no success. Christ could not cure her temper: it was better to leave her alone.

Sadly, the minister had to let her go, discouraged and defeated, and let the next visitor come in. He was a fine, tall man, who had come to make a handsome gift to one of the minister's good causes. He explained why he brought it. 'Six weeks ago,' he said, 'my daughter was converted to Christian life at one of your services; since then the whole atmosphere of our home has changed.' She is so different now, the man continued, everything is different, and the house is happy again. He felt that he just had to show how grateful he was.

The girl, like Peter, was so discouraged that she did not realise how much already God had done in her, but her father saw the difference in her behaviour in six short weeks – just as Jesus saw it in Peter. Discouragement is like that: it always lies to us, making things look worse than they are. Many of God's greatest men have had dark times, when they had to overcome discouragement. Jacob, wrestling with the angel, could only limp afterwards, feeling his weakness. Gideon the mighty soldier confessed 'My family is the weakest, and I am the least in my family.' Elijah protested 'I am no better than my fathers' and pleaded with God to leave him alone. The great Isaiah had once to cry out, 'Woe is me!' And once even Paul had to say, 'I know that in me dwells nothing that is good.'

More often than not we are discouraged because we are so

impatient. We want to see results at once, overnight. But to make a girl, or a lad, strong and true and Christlike, takes time, and patience, and faith in Jesus. He can help us, and he will, not only to do our best but to reach his best, if only we let him take charge.

And one thing we can be sure of: if we really want to follow him, *he will never let us go.*

9 The Clever Old Woman and the Camel

In the middle of London is a great and beautiful public park, and through the park flows a winding river, called (of course) the Serpentine. The park is used by everybody, though it belongs, strictly speaking, to the Queen – it is a royal park. There many people, from many lands, stroll or sit, play games, or admire the flower beds and the great trees. Workpeople go there to eat their lunches; young people walk hand in hand, absorbed (as they ought to be) in each other; children romp and shout to their hearts' content.

It's all great fun, exciting, and healthy, and free. But it belongs to the Queen.

Some years ago an old lady could be found sitting on one of the benches, holding a pretty little basket full of apples which she offered now and again to the children playing near. Sometimes their mothers and fathers felt grateful to the kind old lady, and dropped a coin into her basket to say 'Thank you'. In time, this became the custom, and presently, to be fair to everyone alike, the old lady chose her apples as nearly as possible the same size and charged everyone for them, just a penny or two. It was the Queen's park, not a market. But then the old lady was cheerful and clean and red-cheeked, and no one thought she was doing any harm.

But apples are not cheap all through the year, and sometimes she could not get apples at all, and had to turn the children away. She did not like doing that, so she thought of making sweets instead, and on colder days, she brought warm buns wrapped up in her basket. Still, she was very careful, and did things the right way. She wrote and explained to her Majesty's Master of the Parks (or whatever he was called) just how it was about the apples, and asked permission to offer the children something else instead. He was a very busy man, and passed the letter to someone else, less busy and less important; and *he* could not see much difference between apples

31

and buns if you were offering the children anything at all. So he said 'Yes, of course you can.' And she did.

The lady's name, by the way, was Ann Hicks, and the story is quite true. Everyone passing through Hyde Park got to know her, and the children used to coax their parents around her corner of the path, until she became quite busy. But that brought a problem, too. So Ann wrote another letter to the Queen's Master of the Parks, explaining how hard it was to carry her apples and buns (and toffee and sweets) to the park every day; and could she not leave some overnight in a box which she would provide, with a lock and all. That would save her tired arms and her old back and her weary legs. And the Master of the Parks – who was a kind man as well as busy – said he supposed it would be all right, if she kept it tidy. But when the box came, it was rather big, and the lid was at the side like a door, much more like a small shed than a box. But there it was.

Eating warm buns can make you thirsty. So another letter had to be sent, asking permission to sell ginger-beer with her buns. The good man this time felt a little impatient, and said yes, anything to get this old woman off his back! Which was not very polite, but was very convenient. Only, quite soon, another letter came (for Mrs Hicks did everything properly): 'the ginger-beer bottles are being made too tall to stand on the little shelf with the buns and the apples and the toffee; would it be all right to raise the roof of her lock-up just enough to give them room?'

'Yes, of course' came the reply. And when a workman came to do it, Ann suggested it would be nice if she could stand in out of the rain. So it was made just as high as she was, about five feet. All then went well, and quiet, until the winter, when the rain grew heavy. Water began to trickle in through the shed roof and spoil the buns. Off went yet another letter, asking permission just to put on a few weather-proof tiles, and back came the answer, shorter than ever, saying something like 'O.K.'. More workmen arrived, and these liked Ann's buns and her ginger-beer so much that they gladly agreed with her, that when you are putting on tiles you might as well put in a chimney; and if there was to be a stove, then a window to help clear any smoke would be a great advantage.

Little by little, step by step, taking her time, the little, clever old lady had made herself a tiny home, with a shop window, right in the middle of the Queen's park. It even had a name over the door, 'White Cottage'.

All went well, until someone thought of using the park, with the Queen's permission, for a great exhibition, and important people came to measure and plan and decide where everything was to go, and to their astonishment found standing there, right in their way, in the Queen's own park, a shop! And one for which no rent was ever paid!

Of course they told Ann she had to go – at once. But clever Ann Hicks did not only write letters, she kept them by her, and she could show she had permission for everything she had done: and no one could turn her out. There was a great fuss then, of course; the papers wrote about it, and questions were asked of the Queen's ministers in Parliament: but there she was, and her shop, with official permission, though no one had ever *intended* a shop to be built in the Queen's Park.

Where does the camel come in? you ask: the true answer is, under the tent flap – but that is another, older story. A man tied his camel to a palm tree, went into his tent and settled down to sleep. But the camel was lonely, and cold, and would not rest. It began grumbling, as camels do, and making odd, disturbing noises, until the man got up and opened the tent door. The camel put his nose into the warm tent and was quiet: so the man let him stay, and lay down again. But the camel was soon restless again, and when the man got up and opened the door to push it out, the camel instead got his front feet and his long neck inside, and went quiet. Only for a while – soon his hump was inside the tent, then his back legs, and finally his tail. By morning, the camel was all inside the tent, and the man outside in the cold.

Little sins, little steps towards wrong, do not seem to matter at the time: but they build up marvellously into great wrongs. Things you never at all intended to happen, do come to pass – because we think the little dishonesty, the little gambling, the little swear-words, the little strong drink, do not count. Before we know it they can take possession – with our unintentional permission – and we find ourselves with a problem, and out in the cold.

10 Pippa

Pippa was a young Italian girl who worked in a silk mill except on her one whole day's holiday, which was New Year's Day. Rising early in the lovely sunshine, happy as any girl could be, she tried to plan her free day, not to waste a single precious hour. She was too poor to travel anywhere: she was even called 'that little ragged girl'; but that did not stop her dreaming of wonderful things to do.

She decided to spend the day imagining herself to be, one after the other, the four happiest people in the town. She thought first of Ottima, the wealthy wife of the owner of the silk mill, who had dancing attendance upon her a devoted young lover – not right, of course, but so romantic! She thought next of a young bride, Phene, who was to be married at midday. Then she thought of Luigi, a fine boy, and his loving mother, who lived quietly together in happy companionship. Pippa herself lived alone, and envied Luigi. And then she remembered one thing that was to happen that day, the visit to the town of a very important churchman, to comfort and help the family of his dead brother. Pippa (who had no difficulty dreaming odd things!), said to herself,

> 'I, tonight at least,
> Would be that holy and beloved priest.'

But she did not plan to stay indoors and imagine herself happy: she would take a long, long walk in the sunshine, 'pass by and see their happiness', thinking as she went how nice it would be to share their joy. And she would sing all day. It was quite a plan.

But, though Pippa did not know it, just as she set out for Ottima's fine house, a dreadful quarrel was going on there. For together Ottima and her lover have killed her husband, the mill-owner, and are feeling dreadfully guilty and afraid.

Ottima was trying to persuade her lover just to forget it, not to care what the rest of the world would think about it, but to let all be as it used to be between them. Ottima was arguing in the usual silly way, that the horrible murder did not really matter if they truly 'loved' each other: but just then, outside the palace window, Pippa passed, singing

> The year's at the spring
> And day's at the morn;
> Morning's at seven,
> The hillside's dew pearled;
> The lark's on the wing,
> The snail's on the thorn,
> God's in his heaven –
> All's right with the world.

That changed everything. Her song stabbed the conscience of the wicked young man –

> 'that little peasant's voice
> Has righted all again'

– and in great remorse, he killed himself.

Still not knowing what had happened, Pippa passed on to the house of the bridegroom and his bride, and here too something strange was going on. For the new marriage had really been a horrible trick. Some student friends of the bridegroom had played a cruel prank, pretending that the girl, Phene, had sent loving letters to him, which they themselves had written. The young man's tender replies, with the help of the students and a rather nasty aunt, had led on to the marriage, though Phene never wanted it, and the boy had been deceived. The story is all very complicated and improbable; but now the girl tries to explain, very honestly and brokenheartedly, what has been done. Of course the bridegroom is very, very angry: his marriage is a mess from the first hour.

Again unaware of the truth, Pippa passes beneath the window, thinking how happy the bride must be, and still singing. This time it is of a beautiful Queen who for the sake of true love left her home in Cyprus, and her throne, to come to Italy – a well-known story which enshrined for ordinary good people the kind of love and faithfulness which ought to exist in marriage. As he listened, the young bridegroom's heart was touched, and he looked with altogether new kindness on his

young bride of an hour. Thinking of the song, he determined that, however they had come to be married, he was going to make her happy – they would be happy together.

Passing on, Pippa came to a turret, where Luigi and his mother sat talking together. A terrible duty has been laid upon the young man, to take action in revolt against a wicked king. It is exceedingly dangerous, and Luigi hesitates. His mother argues with him, pleading that he should leave such work to others, or to another day, or abandon it altogether. She speaks to him of her love, and of the love of someone else he hoped to see in months to come – all at risk if he goes on this dangerous errand. Luigi almost gives in, but in the street below, Pippa passes, still singing.

The song recalls old kings of ancient times, just and good, loving their people and protected by the gods. As he listens, Luigi hears in the song the summons to do his duty, in spite of danger, to restore the freedom of the people from a wicked ruler, and make way for a good king like those of old. Pippa's song has given him courage – though she knows nothing of that.

In the evening Pippa came to the house of sadness, where the good old priest has arrived to help and comfort. But here yet again something was going on of which she could know nothing. The dead brother has been very wicked, and now to save losing a lot of money and lands, the priest is being sorely tempted by his brother's old steward, to take part in further wickedness. Or, if he will not do that, to let someone else do it, and keep silent. Once more Pippa passes at the right moment, singing this time of the beauty of the world, of the innocence of childhood, and the goodness of God. The old priest hears, and comes to his senses – or to his conscience. Immediately he rejects the whole evil scheme and exposes the truth.

So Pippa returned home, tired but happy; and as she prepared for bed, too weary (she said) to pray more than 'God bless me', she wondered how near she had come to all these people she had dreamed of being. She wondered, too, if she could possibly in some way have done them good, or harm. She laughed at herself, sleepily, for supposing that she could have any such importance, and then remembered a line from her morning song –

    All service is the same with God

– and fell asleep.

One day you will read the full story of Pippa in a rather difficult poem by Robert Browning: it is worth struggling with. All unknown to herself, Pippa had brought one man to repent an evil deed, taught two young people to love each other, given to a young hero greater courage, and saved an old man from temptation – just by singing her way, simply and innocently, through her holiday.

> God make my life a Happy song,
>   That comforteth the sad,
> That helpeth others to be strong
>   And makes the singer glad.
>
> God make my life a tuneful hymn,
>   Of tenderness and praise,
> Of faith that never waxes dim
>   In all his wondrous ways.

11 The Best Looking Girl in Cappadocia

That is a nice thing to have said about you – provided you live in Cappadocia, of course. And it was said by her brother: not many brothers talk about their sisters in that complimentary way.

The girl's name was Macrina, and she lived in a great house by the river Isis, near the Black Sea, as wealthy as she was beautiful. She might have married anyone she chose, and in fact engaged herself to marry a splendid young lawyer. But he died, and Macrina felt she could not love anyone else in the same way; so she remained unmarried.

Instead, she gave herself to study, to reading, and to prayer. To study was unusual for a girl in those days, about three hundred years after Jesus, but Macrina was educated and clever, learning long Bible passages by heart, including the whole of the Psalms – all one hundred and fifty of them.

The reason for Macrina's strong faith and love of prayer is interesting. Her grandmother, also called Macrina, was a Christian heroine. During the last years of persecution of Christians by the Roman Emperors, grandmother and grandfather had escaped, leaving their lovely home to seek safety among the mountains. For seven years they moved from hiding-place to hiding-place, narrowly eluding their pursuers, but never willing to give up their Christian faith. Only when they were allowed to be Christians and safe, did they return to their home.

Macrina, the grand-daughter, knew that story, and honoured the name she inherited. But in spite of her beauty, her wealth, her cleverness and her faith, all was not easy for her. She grieved, of course, for her lost sweetheart, and also very soon afterwards for her father. When her father died, her mother was not well enough, or wise enough, to take over the management and business affairs of the great house and lands, and care for the large family, nine children in all. So Macrina took charge.

Besides the business work, organising the farms and caring for the tenants and the work-people, Macrina looked after the house, taught the children, cared for them in sickness; and as her mother grew older, Macrina herself prepared all her food, baked her bread, and tended her devotedly. Always it was Macrina who had to be wise, who took decisions, who got things done. Not content with all this, Macrina went on thinking, studying, writing, and gained something of a reputation as a Christian teacher throughout the district.

With her brothers and sisters to bring up, and to teach, Macrina needed to know what she was talking about. The result of her work for them shows plainly how very successful she was, for no less than *three* of the boys became famous as leaders in the church, bishops organising and training large numbers of workers for Christ, and caring for many Christian people.

One was Peter, a bishop in Palestine, whom Macrina had trained right from babyhood. Another was later known everywhere as Saint Gregory, a very famous teacher and writer of the early church, whose books are still studied. It was he who wrote his sister's life story, remembering how much he owed to her, recording much of her conversation. It was he, too, who called her the best looking girl in Cappadocia. And, perhaps a higher compliment still, in his own writings, even on serious and difficult subjects, Gregory does not mind admitting how much he learned from his eldest sister.

The third very famous brother was Saint Basil, usually called 'the Great' – though Gregory insisted that it was Macrina who should be called 'great'. In those days, Christians often shut themselves away from the busy life of the world, living alone as monks and nuns to give their lives wholly to study and to prayer. Basil was one of the first to show that this was not Christ's way. 'God has made us like members of a body', so Basil taught, 'to need one another's help. For what discipline of humility, or pity, or patience can there be, if there be none with us to whom these duties are to be done? Whose feet will you wash, whom will you serve, how can you be (as Jesus said) "least of all", if you are all

alone? He who lives for himself may have a precious gift, but he buries it. Whoever knows Christ's parable of the talents must know how great a responsibility it is to bury in idleness what God has given you to use.'

In time, the whole church came to listen to Basil, and returned from selfish piety to Christ's way of service and love towards and amongst others: but when Basil said these things he was most unpopular, and sharply criticised. Where then did he learn to think that way? It happens that we know the answer.

For when, after long study abroad, Basil returned home, he was already famous as a learned man, a fine speaker and a powerful writer. But he was dreadfully conceited, looking contemptuously on all the local leaders in the church, thinking himself far better than all the teachers in his home district. Macrina saw this, and took her brother firmly in hand, clever and famous though he was. She taught him to think in more Christian ways, persuaded him to follow and imitate Jesus, and won him for Christ's true service. As Gregory tells us, Basil gave away his fortune, and left behind all his former fame and conceit 'for this busy life where one toils with one's hands'.

But 'this busy life where one toils with one's hands' is exactly what Basil was to teach the whole church about Christian service – that study and prayer are meant to fit us to *work* for other people and for Christ.

It was his busy, active, studying, praying, estate-managing, child-rearing, cooking, toiling, devoted sister, Macrina, who made Basil see what Jesus meant when he said, 'If you know these things, happy are you if you DO them', and again, 'Not everyone who says to me "Lord, Lord" shall enter the kingdom of heaven, but he who DOES the will of my Father...'

The best looking girl in Cappadocia had done her work well.

12 He Lifted Her Up

I

'Mary' is a beautiful name, which is why so many girls possess it. This Mary lived in Jerusalem in the time of Jesus, and though we know but little about her, it is all good.

We never hear of her husband, and the home she lived in is spoken of as hers, so it seems likely her husband had died. Yet she was not alone, for a splendid son, whom we all know about and honour, lived with her. This was John Mark, friend of Paul, and of Barnabas, and very famous himself later on, as writer of one of the gospels. The house in Jerusalem was fairly large, with a fine guest room for special occasions. Mary had a servant-girl, too, named Rhoda. So it would seem that Mary was fairly well-off.

Much more important, she was a good friend of Jesus and useful to him. On the last night of his life, just before he was crucified, Jesus wished to spend some hours in safety, shut in with his disciples, undisturbed and yet within the city. There was a price upon his head, and to give him shelter was dangerous: yet with real courage and love, Mary had arranged for her home to be open to him, and she promised to get ready that large upper guest room, with tables and rugs set, where he and the twelve could eat the Passover.

It was all pre-arranged, and very hush-hush. Not even the disciples were told whether Jesus would stay within the city, or where. Instead two were separated from the rest (and so from Judas, watching his opportunity to betray Jesus), and sent ahead to follow a man carrying a water-pot – woman's work, usually – and he would lead them to the right place. The rest, including Judas, only learned where it was when they arrived with Jesus. Before the night was through, after Judas had left to tell the authorities where Jesus was, Jesus left Mary's house and went to the garden of Gethsemane, lest the soldiers should arrest him in Mary's home, and perhaps arrest her too. There, in the garden, young John Mark tried to warn Jesus, ahead of Judas, and was nearly arrested himself.

In spite of continuing danger, that guest room in Mary's house became for a while the headquarters of the church in Jerusalem. There the disciples gathered after Jesus' ascension, and there they still were meeting for prayer when Peter, released from prison, came looking for them. Christian girls should be proud of Mary of Jerusalem, the mother of John Mark, who opened her home to Jesus in dangerous days.

II

Priscilla was a business-woman, travelling and working along-side her husband, Aquila, a Jew from Asia Minor. They were tent-makers, or perhaps leather-workers, or both. Their business seems to have stretched from Rome to Corinth, and even to Ephesus. We know that some sixteen years after Jesus died, trouble arose in the synagogues at Rome, apparently over the claim that Jesus was the Christ, the Messiah. As a result, many Jews were banished from the city by the Emperor, and among them were Aquila and Priscilla. So they came to the great Greek seaport of Corinth, a city with an evil reputation for vice and violence and all sorts of crime.

Later, when they move on with Paul to Ephesus, we find (very unusually for those days) that Priscilla is often mentioned before her husband: it seems unlikely that among Christians that could be because she was of higher rank; more probably she was the stronger character, or the cleverer, of the two. At Ephesus, these two take in hand the better instruction of young Apollos, a brilliant man, eloquent, persuasive, well trained in scripture, but not yet understanding the gospel of the Lord Jesus very well. Priscilla and Aquila set about explaining things to him more clearly: that says something of Apollos' willingness to learn – and even more about their ability to teach such a man.

Paul's ministry at Corinth was a stormy one. Driven by opposition out of the synagogue, accused by enemies before the Roman governor of Corinth, he was for a time in the greatest danger. In addition, the wicked manners and evil reputation of the city made it very hard for new converts to hold fast to Christ. It was almost a test-place for the gospel – could it achieve anything in so vile a city; it was certainly a test for Paul – could he win coverts there, stay on, outface the enmity, and establish a living church?

Paul did stay, for at least a year and a half. All that time, his closest friends and supporters were Priscilla and Aquila. In their home he lived – certainly at first, and probably for the whole time of his stay, though the Christians met for worship in another, probably larger, house. So another woman opened her house to the servant of Christ, and in this instance that had special importance. It made it possible for Paul to demonstrate for all time the power of Jesus to save men and women even in the worst situations. Christian girls should be proud of Priscilla, who opened the world's worst city to the gospel of Christ.

III

Lydia, too, was a business-woman, from a town called Thyatira in what is now Turkey. (To be quite accurate, we are not absolutely certain that 'Lydia' was her personal name; it may have been meant for 'the Lydian lady', for Thyatira was in the district of Lydia; perhaps 'Lydian' was a nickname). Lydia's business was selling a famous dye which came from her home district, and when we meet her she is many miles from home, in Philippi.

Lydia was already a devout woman, often meeting with other women for prayer at a place appointed along the riverside near the city. To that praying group Paul and his companions joined themselves when they first reached Philippi, and it was to them that the story of Jesus and the message of salvation was first told, in all that region.

A lovely thing is said of this devout, and successful business-woman. 'The Lord opened her heart to give heed to what was said by Paul, and when she was baptized with her household she besought us, saying, "If you have judged me to be faithful to the Lord, come to my house and stay".'

And so another home was opened to the Christian message. But here there is even more. Philippi was the very first point at which the Christian gospel reached and entered Europe: hitherto it had been preached (so far as history tells) only in

Asia and the east. Thus Lydia is the first Christian in Europe – a woman – and her home was the birthplace of the church in Europe. Christian girls should be proud of Lydia, whose heart the Lord opened, and who opened a whole continent for Christ.

IV

But then, these are only a few of the women who have foremost place in the New Testament story. Women waited upon Jesus during his ministry and supported him with gifts; Mary Magdalene, and Martha and Mary of Bethany were among his most faithful disciples. Jesus healed and spoke to women at least as often as he ministered to men. Women were the last to leave him at the cross, held there by their love and loyalty; and they were the first at his grave, when the Sabbath had passed, and first therefore to find that he had risen again. Mary, Jesus' mother, has a special place in Christian affection, for Jesus' sake.

Women, like men, were promised the gift of the Spirit, that 'your daughters and your handmaidens' should prophesy – as Philip's four daughters did. Women like Phebe at Cenchrea were deaconesses in the scattered churches that apostles founded. During the years of fierce persecution, women were at least as steadfast, as courageous, as faithful unto death, as ever the men were: we know scores of their names and the stories of their martyrdom.

Christian girls should always be proud of the place of women in the Christian story. In his gospel, John Mark tells how Jesus approached one woman, who was sick of fever, saying that 'He took her by the hand and lifted her up'. Luke, too, has a moving record of Jesus coming upon a woman who was bent, hump-backed, looking always upon the ground because she was unable to lift herself up. Luke says Jesus spoke kindly to her, and set her free of her deformity, so that she could lift her head, walk upright, and look the whole world in the face. Both Mark and Luke understood how very much women, in that ancient world, owed to the love and care of Jesus: he had brought to them a new dignity, a new freedom, a new hope and joy, as daughters of the living God.

In very truth, 'He lifted her up'.

13 A Fragrant Tale

A lovely story is told about the little village of Luss, in Scotland. But then, Luss itself is a lovely place, just one short street and a main road, nestling beside Loch Lomond, with a short pier that juts over the water for the loch steamer to call in summertime. Inland from Luss runs a marvellous narrow glen, with only one little winding road that climbs higher and higher between tall hedges and trees until at the very top you can look back to the shining water of the loch, the circle of high hills around it, and the scattering of islands, and feel you are looking down upon the world.

But the one main street is lovely in itself – the pier at one end, a great sheltering tree at the other, the cottages small and beautifully kept, each opening almost on to the road with the smallest pavement you ever saw, just big enough to stand the milk-bottle on each morning. And along each house front, and on the window sills and around the doors, and hanging from the door lintels and the corners of each roof, are — *flowers*.

In summer, Luss is filled with flowers, thousands of them, of every kind you ever saw and some of them you might never see, except in Luss. And that is the story, as it is sometimes told to visitors.

Little boats ply among the islands in the shining loch, and can take you to one quite famous in local history. It contains a monk's cell, deserted now and ruined, but long the home of a saintly man revered and loved throughout the district as 'Saint' Kessog. He was (we are told) a good and kindly man, wise in his counsel, a friend to all in trouble, a willing teacher of all who came to him, so that the fragrance of his life and faith filled the lochside villages.

Long ago, Luss had another name, Clachan Dubh, which means the dark, or gloomy, hamlet. This (it is said to strangers) was because plague once swept the cottages, bringing disease and death to every family. In those days, perhaps around AD 500, Kessog lived alone in his island cell, studied hard, said his prayers, helped all he could, and dreamed of travel. For, like many Christians of his time, Kessog longed to visit other lands, some say, to go to Palestine, others say, to visit centres of Christian learning in Europe. Either journey would be costly and dangerous, and he kept putting it off, but as years went by his desire grew, and at last he set out.

Through Scotland and northern England he travelled nearly always on foot, but sometimes helped forward in other ways by Christians whom he visited, so coming in time to France and Italy. How far he went is not said, but he seems to have returned through Spain, for there the dangers of travel caught up with him. He was set upon, robbed, and killed.

The sad news took a long time to reach Luss, but when it came it cast gloom over all the woods and hillsides and farmlands for miles around. The cell stood empty, for no one seemed worthy to take Kessog's place. Whether the plague happened after this, or before he left home, is not clear, but presently the feeling grew that if the village really desired God's blessing, something should be done about bringing Kessog's body home. Sharing the cost between them, the villagers sent off messengers to where their 'saint' had been reverently laid by Spanish Christians, to beg that he might be brought back to Loch Lomond and his own people.

So eventually, Kessog was buried in a private chapel near Clachan Dubh; later his stone coffin was removed to the churchyard by the loch. But those who in Spain had shown kindness to Kessog had done their work well. His body had been carefully cleansed and anointed with sweet oils, then wrapped in Spanish silks with spices and sweet herbs and fragrant flowers in every fold. And – so the lovely story tells – as loving hands carried Kessog through the village in procession to his grave, the seeds of spices, herbs and flowers were scattered accidentally through the street and the lane and in the chapel, to spread later into every garden and hedgerow, along the glen and across the fields.

So Kessog had brought a new kind of fragrance to the village he had loved, like the fragrance of his life and memory. 'Clachan Dubh' was changed to 'Luss', which (we are told) meant 'herb-flower-garden'; and the tradition grew up that everyone who came to live in Luss must keep the flowers blooming in memory of the 'saint'. *That* is why Luss is still one of the loveliest villages in Scotland.

Exactly how true it all is, no one knows, but it recalls two other stories worth remembering, both even older, and one certainly true.

One is the tale of Joseph of Arimathea, the man who helped to bury Jesus. It was said that when the Romans destroyed Jerusalem, Joseph travelled first to France, as a missionary, and then on to England, which was of course still pagan. He landed somewhere in Cornwall, and came on the day before Christmas to the beautiful island of Avalon, now Glastonbury, in Somerset. Here he and his companions rested, in a little wattle hut beside the river. But before he slept, Joseph set upright in the ground his heavy staff of thorn-wood, which he had brought all the way from Palestine, and said 'Here I will build a church'.

When he awoke on Christmas morning, the staff had blossomed, in honour of the birthday of Jesus! In time it grew into a great bush, and nearby was built the first church in England, small, of mud and branches, but later to become the great and beautiful Abbey of Glastonbury.

Of course there is argument about this old story too. A thorn-tree which flowers at Christmas is still there, and I have heard that the Queen has had a flowering twig from it upon her Christmas dinner-table. But the other story, though still older, is certainly true. It tells how a woman in the house at Bethany anointed the feet of Jesus with costly perfumed ointment, in homage and in love; and it mentions how the fragrance of the ointment filled all the house where they were sitting. And Jesus said that to the end of time, wherever his gospel was preached, the story of her fragrant love would be told and retold in her memory.

'How sweet the name of Jesus sounds' – and how fragrant is the memory of all those who have loved him dearly and served him well!

14 To Be Free!

A young slave boy was hurrying through the streets of the crowded city: it may have been Rome, it could have been Ephesus, but he was certainly in trouble.

To be a slave at all was bad enough. It meant long hard hours of work, without wages, without a home of his own to go to afterwards, since he lived in his master's home, always on call. He *belonged* to his master, as the horses, the pigs, the kitchen pots, belonged to him. And it must always be so, he must always be someone's slave, as long as he lived. But he did so long to be free.

Free people had families, and homes, and friends, people who loved them; they could marry, have children, keep them and watch them grow; they could visit other people, play games, save up, enjoy life. Slaves could do only what the master allowed. If they married, and had children, it was only for so long as the master chose – the wife, and the children, were his to sell. A slave's baby was a good profit to the master: perhaps that is how this slave had received his name, Onesimus, meaning 'profitable'. No wonder a slave longed to be free!

But how? A few slaves earned freedom by some special service to a good master, saving his life, rescuing a child; but you might wait all your life for a chance like that. The only way to gain freedom was to run for it – act free, pretend you are free, assert your freedom and go! This is what our slave had done. He just ran away, he was free!

But to run away with nothing in your pocket made no sense. You would not get far, and you would soon be hungry. Very quickly you would have to beg, or steal, to stay alive. Far better to take something with you, and if you have nothing, then you might as well steal before you start. Onesimus had evidently thought that out, and stolen something before he ran. Now he felt really free. No one could call him to do things, order him about, beat him if he was slow or made mistakes; there was no work always waiting to be done. With money in his pocket he could travel where he wished, hire a room, buy what he fancied – he was free!

Then why was he hurrying, furtively, hugging the shadows, keeping to the side streets? One reason was that every runaway slave was up against the law. All free people were supposed to notice runaways, and report them or arrest them. Slaves must be kept in their place, and responsible citizens must help to find them and restore them to their masters.

But how would anyone recognise a runaway slave? – by marks cut in his face, or shoulders, or hands, his master's ownership marks, like initials on the side of a sheep, or registration numbers on a car. Most people of course might never notice a strange slave with strange marks in their district, but when they were asked to rent him a room or sell him food, then just as garages today would soon notice a foreign car number, so business people would quickly note a slave who did not belong to any of the great families of the town, and start asking questions. So a runaway would try to keep out of sight, to avoid people, to stay only at lodging-houses where other 'wanted' people stayed. He was not quite so free after all: he could not go where he liked, or meet free people freely.

Besides, to have stolen from his master made things much worse. If found, he would have to give some explanation for the money he carried, and how he had managed to travel and eat; and if suspected of theft, he could be severely punished – even put to death.

Of course, however much he had stolen, it would not last for ever. To work was impossible, for very few would employ a slave with no master to sell him, or give him away. With hunger, would come thoughts of the household he had left, where even harsh masters saw to it that slaves were fed, so that they could work.

And the runaway would be lonely. He could trust no one, tell his story to no one, but be always on his guard against questions, and against the sort of people who lived where he lived. This 'freedom' did not turn out at all as he expected. Fearful, hunted, lonely, in constant danger, without home or other slaves to talk with, or a bed at night, however poor, that was his own, and soon without regular food, freedom seemed an empty thing. Perhaps if he had thought it all out properly beforehand he would not have longed so desperately to be free.

We would give a great deal to know exactly what happened next, but we cannot be sure. We know that Onesimus met an old man; and as the old man was in prison – 'imprisonment for the gospel' he called it – it seems probable that the slave-lad must also have got himself into prison. Had he stolen again? or been recognised? or got into a fight? If that is true, his 'freedom' had not lasted very long.

And here the story, like all good stories, has an unexpected twist. For the old man in prison knew the lad's master!

That meeting changed everything. First, the old man taught the slave-boy the Christian way to freedom: not by asserting you are free when you are not; not by stealing and running away into trouble; not by rebellion and breaking the law; but by giving over your life to Christ, who loves you, cares for you, died for you. Be sure of that, and it will not much matter who your earthly master is, or what you have to do. *With Christ's peace and joy within your heart,* the old man would tell the runaway, *you are in heart a free man already, with a dignity, a value, and an inner freedom, which no one can take from you.* You are Christ's free man: he makes you free. Stand up in that freedom, and do not bother about being a slave in men's eyes.

Now this was very odd. The old man who talked so much of freedom was himself a prisoner, though he did not seem to mind. He could sing songs in prison, preach in prison, write letters in prison to people all across the Empire. His heart was free, though his body was 'in bonds'. His name (as you have guessed) was Paul. And his attitude, in his circumstances, was living proof to Onesimus that freedom is after all something inside you.

There was more: though Paul was one of the 'free people', and indeed a freeman of the Roman Empire, yet he loved to call himself a slave of Christ, and to call Christ his master. He lived in complete obedience to Jesus, and enjoyed it! He even spoke of the many scars he bore, marks of old injuries received in the service of Christ, as slave-marks of the Lord

Jesus, showing to whom he belonged. And Paul *wanted* it so. He grieved if he disobeyed, and took his own way. Because, Paul would say, Christ had first set him free from the power of sin and the fear of death, he was glad to live now as the bondslave of so loving a Master.

The slave lad must have been very puzzled. No one could be more free in spirit, more happy in heart, than Paul was, yet Paul was not only willing, but over-joyed, to belong to Christ, purchased by his suffering and death, and entirely servant of his will. With it all, Paul was certainly happier than any lonely, fearful, hungry runaway, hiding in the city's back-street lodging houses, could hope to be.

Onesimus was persuaded to try the Christian way to freedom, by surrendering to Jesus. He soon learned that that meant undoing all the wrong he had done. Christians do not pretend wrong does not matter: they put it right. Onesimus must go home to his master, to whom he still belonged, and be a Christian slave. And the stolen money . . . ?

That is where Paul had the Christian answer. He wrote to his friend Philemon, Onesimus' master, a very charming letter which the slave was to carry back home. In it Paul told of the lad's conversion, and pointed out to the master the great difference that made. Paul, an old man, and (as he reminded his friend) a prisoner of the gospel, pleaded for Onesimus a welcome home, not any longer as just a slave, but as a brother, a brother in Christ and a brother for Paul's sake too.

Paul would like to have kept him, as a personal attendant, to do all that he knew Philemon would like to have done for his old friend: but he had thought it better to send him back. Then, if Onesimus did return and serve Paul, it would be his master's free and ready gift. He is now, as a Christian (Paul said) all that his name promised, a 'profitable' servant. 'As for this money – well, if he owes you anything, put it down on my bill. I will pay it. And I will not remind you how much you owe *me*, already, to balance against it!' Paul had evidently led Philemon, too, to Christian life: for that great privilege Philemon owed to Paul much more than Onesimus had stolen, though as Paul says he would not mention such a thing!

And then, along with all the charm and good humour, Paul adds the very slightest of warnings. Just in case Philemon, or any one else, thought it was asking too much to welcome back a runaway slave and forgive him for stealing, Paul mentions that he intends to visit Philemon, and asks for a guest room to be prepared. They will renew friendship soon, at Philemon's table – with Onesimus to wait on them. (And if Onesimus was not there, and happy, Paul would want to know why!)

So it happened. We have the letter in our New Testament. And so Onesimus found the freedom he longed for: freedom from fear, from danger, from loneliness, from homelessness, from guilt; he found a kind master, a secure home, Christian friends, the love of Christ, and all the dignity of a Christian man. He really was free, because like Paul he was the slave of Christ.

Some think that long afterwards Onesimus became a Christian leader, a minister, and finally the bishop of Ephesus. And that he was the very first to collect together the letters of his loved old friend who taught him the true meaning of freedom. I would not be at all surprised if that were true. But that it *could* be true, that a runaway, thieving slave could become a Christian bishop and the first to gather together the books of our New Testament, is part of the wonder of the gospel.

15 Betsy's Imps

Betsy was being teased, and then scolded, by her eleven brothers and sisters. It was a beautiful day, and they were all together in the fine park surrounding their magnificent home in the country. But Betsy would not join in the games. She was serious, and a little troubled. Although only seventeen, she had heard a man speaking of God with such power and persuasiveness that for the first time she was considering what she ought to do with her life.

An attractive girl, with wealth, friends, a beautiful home, a loving and clever family, everything about her that was gentle and good, and the prospect of marriage to a gentle, good man – also very wealthy – she really ought to have been happy. But Betsy was uncertain what she wanted, and unsatisfied with what she had. No wonder her brothers and sisters sometimes called her 'stupid'.

Yet the day would come when a Duke would speak of her 'majestic figure, her dignity and power', and confess that he felt 'awe' in her presence. The King of Prussia would one day come to dinner in her cottage, when she herself had become much poorer. A Princess would come to breakfast, and Betsy would sit between the Prime Minister and a Prince, at London's Mansion House. But meanwhile, she wondered what she ought to be doing with her life.

The first, most obvious thing that she could do was to seek out people, especially children, in the nearby village and offer any help she could. That led swiftly to one boy coming into the great house for lessons – there were few opportunities of education for poor people. He soon brought friends, who brought other friends, until there were seventy very lively children on Sunday evenings in the large attic, all being taught simple reading, sums, and Bible stories. These were, in the family's teasing, 'Betsy's imps'. Yet the brothers and sisters respected Betsy. Said one of them 'I never remember her to have been shaken in one single point which she felt to be her duty.'

For a long time Betsy hesitated about her marriage. It seemed so selfish to think only of her own happiness. Her sweetheart must have been *very* patient! In the end he arranged to leave his watch on a garden seat: if Betsy picked it up to return it, that would mean 'Yes'. He got his watch and his wife.

That meant moving to London, but soon Betsy was visiting the poor around her new home, and giving much of her time to those completely destitute in the great workhouse for the poor at Islington. She planned classes for the children, distributed food, clothes, and medicines, and began to be especially interested in those thrown into prison for robbery, picking pockets, violence, debt, madness, or murder. This deep and strange concern was not new to her, for at fifteen she had accompanied her father on a visit to a 'House of Correction' at Norwich, and had been horrified. Three hundred women, with their children, lived in two wards and two cells, with only one tap between them, in terrible conditions of squalor and disease. Most became wilder and more ungovernable, the longer they stayed in prison.

In those days, one hundred and sixty years ago, criminals of all ages, the very poor and the mad were all herded together in the most dreadful filth and over-crowding, without proper food or clothes or medical care – men, women, children together in unlit, unheated cells, without bedding, and with nothing at all to do. Hundreds died of starvation, or of horrible diseases, spread by dirt, discomfort, and neglect. Those who could beg money became drunken, and many fights and riots broke out. Even the jailers were usually afraid to enter the prisons, and only kept any sort of order by bullying. Very many of the prisoners were simply put to death, some allowed to die, hundreds transported to Australia, never to see their homes again. In London, Betsy – or Mrs Elisabeth Fry as she should now be called – saw things far worse than she had seen in Norwich, or could ever have imagined.

She was distressed most of all for the children, growing up without home, or love, or care, or any chance of a better life later on. But her own family was increasing (she had eleven children), and some family bereavements, and another change of house, kept her very busy, in addition to organising a school, helping to nurse the sick, running a food-kitchen for the very poor near her new home, and sometimes speaking in her Christian meeting – for she had been persuaded by others to preach the gospel.

Yet when a Frenchman from America, visiting England to study the condition of the poor, came to tell Elisabeth of the dreadful things he had seen in the streets and the prisons of London, saying 'Surely something *must* be done!' Elisabeth immediately sent out to the shops for flannel, and a message around her young women friends. The very next day Elisabeth called at Newgate prison with bundles of quickly made warm clothes for the women and children. Three such visits were possible before she had to leave London again for a time: but as soon as she returned, she began again.

But by that time she had thought and thought, and something much bigger was in her mind. It was not enough to hand out clothes and go home: first she must make the prisoners *accept her as a friend*.

The story of Elisabeth's visit to Newgate prison has been told many times, though it is dreadful to hear. After some argument with the prison governor, who was afraid the women prisoners would attack her, and rob her of her simple but good clothing, Elisabeth insisted upon walking in alone, wearing her watch to show she trusted them, and without protection. At first the prisoners were astonished at such a lady coming among them: then they surged forward all round her, and that moment was full of peril. In one corner, a grey-haired old woman was screeching a very rough song and drinking spirits; in another, two women were fighting, clawing each other's bleeding faces; in yet another place a woman lay moaning on the dirty straw, very ill with jail-fever. The least sign of fear, or of recoil from the awful sounds and smells, and the poor wretches might leap upon Elisabeth in envious anger. Quietly standing, Elisabeth gazed around, looking for some thing she could do to touch their hearts, and saw two women stripping a dead child to use the rags he wore for another boy, four or five years old.

At once Elisabeth moved towards that dirty, shrunken little

boy, lifted him to her arms, and said 'Friends, many of you are mothers – so am I. Isn't there something we can do for these little ones?' As if by magic, the mood changed, a few women wept, someone pushed forward a broken chair, all tried to tell her their sad stories. They brought to her their children, and they pleaded for any help she could give. By the end of that afternoon, her big scheme was already begun.

Elisabeth had started something that was to change prisons not only in England but in Scotland, Ireland, France, Denmark, Holland, Germany, Russia and Australia.

It is a long, long story. Elisabeth's plan was simple, and yet daring. No one else believed it could ever be done. She wanted in each prison a school to help the children prepare for a useful, happier life in freedom. She planned that some of the women should themselves be teachers. All kinds of difficulties were put in her way – no room, no books, no wish to learn, no discipline possible in prison, but Elisabeth would listen to none of them. Very quickly, many of the prisoners themselves cleared rooms, scrubbed floors and planks, tidied the children, encouraged all the way, and triumphed over everything. *Within three months*, 'Newgate School' was known throughout the country; within three years, Elisabeth was writing about it, visiting and advising, all over Europe.

Soon sewing circles were organised within the prison, with the prisoners being taught, first to make and to repair their own clothes, and then to make things for sale – sixty to a hundred pairs of stockings a month, twenty thousand articles within a year! Next Elisabeth became engaged in constant writing, speaking at public meetings, addressing important committees, even attending Parliament to oppose the execution of women, the use of chains in prison, the transporting of mothers to Australia, and then to oppose the sending away of any women at all.

Her writings were translated; the Queen invited her to the palace; the American Ambassador visited her work to report to his President; all ranks of people consulted her. In the midst of her busy life, a poor lad was found frozen to death on her own doorstep – and *within six hours* Elisabeth had organised a shelter for homeless children of the street. Soon she and her helpers were caring for two hundred every night.

The story goes on and on. There seemed to be no end to her energy and her ideas, nor to her influence, nor to her love. The serious, 'stupid' younger sister, against all expectation and in the midst of enormous obstacles, had accomplished tremendous things in the care of the poor, in responsibility towards children, and in the way the world deals with its criminals and with the insane.

Yet at the end she could say, 'My temptation has always been to take things too easily.'

Whew!

And Elisabeth's favourite text: 'Lord, I believe: help thou mine unbelief.'

16 Show A Light There!

Two campers sat late into the evening by the great Hudson River in northern Canada. It was a hot June night, and the fireflies were dancing like a miniature cloud of tiniest stars, in, out, up, down, round, an endless maze of moving sparks in the gathering gloom. Watching closely, one of the campers noticed that every now and then one of the sparks flared briefly into brilliant light and went out again.

Calling the attention of his friend, he asked if this meant that the firefly was exhausted, or whether perhaps it had just died. 'On the contrary,' his friend replied, 'it means that it is safe. You see, other insects are watching this dancing, larger ones, and swifter ones, which you and I cannot see only because the light is so poor. But the fireflies can see them. Each time a larger insect darts in to pick off its prey amid the swirl, the firefly being chased flares its light and actually scares its enemy, or possibly just dazzles it. So it gets away. Any fly that fails to let its light shine will surely die before the night is done.'

That scrap of a story came back to my mind as I sat over coffee with a young lad in the United States Air Force. He seemed exceptionally young, even for a cadet: perhaps the more so because he was very, very upset. He had good reason to be.

The lad was being sent home in disgrace, dismissed his cadetship, losing his opportunity in the Air Force he loved, and having to face home and parents with a confession. He told me a sorry story of homesickness, and loneliness, and temptation. He had learned to drink, and to play cards, and that had led to other things better left alone, which he could not afford. In the end, to pay for his pleasures and his debts, he had stolen, had been found out, and so was dismissed. It was all over now, and settled; he would leave for home in a day or so. He felt extremely sorry for himself – though, to his credit, he offered no excuses, and he blamed no one but himself.

But why come to me? We had never met before. Did he want me to plead on his behalf, to try to get him off? No, it was too late, and anyhow, Air Force Cadet discipline was very strict. Then why had he come? His Commanding Officer advised him to seek me out. This was more puzzling still: what was I supposed to do?

It came out eventually that the lad was from a fine Christian home, and he had been, if not actually a member, at any rate a regular attender of a church like my own. All his friends at home were good Christian people; his background, his character, his recommendations when he joined up were splendid. So, although discipline had to be maintained, and the rules had to be obeyed, yet the Commanding Officer felt deeply sorry for the boy. He did not want him to go completely to pieces. He thought that a minister might be able to help the lad to handle this disappointment and disgrace, and to learn something useful from the experience. Above all, the Commanding Officer wanted the boy to learn that one bad mistake was not the end of life.

So I tried, though in fact the boy had already learned his lesson. I enquired if, since arriving in Britain, he had visited any of our churches, fearing that perhaps he had not been welcomed. No, he had not visited any church: Back home, he said, he had gone to church so often that he thought he would like a change, especially as his free time was limited.

The other thing that could have helped to keep him straight was good friendship. Had he not found Christian friends in camp, to stand by him, and help him resist temptation? No, he had not sought for any. In fact, he did not let anyone know that he was a Christian. He had wanted to go his own way, and not feel all the time that he must behave as a follower of Christ.

His present disgrace was the almost inevitable outcome of that attitude: those who fail to let their light shine soon fall victims to their enemies.

Compare with that young American airman in peacetime, another Christian, taken prisoner during war time. He had seen how, in his Japanese concentration camp, under the stress of captivity, people were beginning to behave badly. Normally kindly people became irritable and discourteous; rudeness and selfishness quickly increased; fights broke out as men strove only for their own comfort or for the little food available. Stealing became almost the accepted way of getting more, with inevitable distrust and anger; and even worse habits of impurity and viciousness crept in – altogether, prison-camp life is so boring, depressing and hopeless that it can bring out the worst in most people.

Seeing all this, the Christian thought a lot about what he could do to help men be their best, and make the camp as cheerful and tolerable as possible. He took care about his own behaviour, but that was not enough; and lecturing or preaching to fellow-prisoners was not going to be welcomed. Instead he began to paint, in the Chinese style, pictures of camp life, making up a series of cartoons – like the strip cartoons in comics – all telling the story of a funny little man, rather helpless, gentle, lovable, and very, very funny.

Each time the Christian noticed something being done in camp that was dishonourable, or unkind, or cruel, he would show that being done to his little man, and how cheerfully the little man would take it, how cleverly he would react to it – and always, somehow, come out on top. How the little man's dinner was eaten by a bully, but because of his cheerfulness all the prisoners round him gave him half a spoonful – which made so much he could not eat it. And how by simply pretending to be very deaf, the little man just did not hear the awful threats and insults which the camp's worst character flung at him, but went on shaking hands and smiling until everybody in sight was laughing.

Of course it was all much more funny to *see* than to tell about, and very soon, as each new picture was pinned on a wall, the prisoners crowded round to enjoy it and point out details to each other. And then, often, to go away still chuckling, but thoughtful. Just occasionally the pictures would remind them of the need for faith in God, and hope for the future; I think that now and again the picture was just a lovely scene. These are the things that keep people *sane* in all kinds of situations – beauty, kindness, laughter and faith: and it worked in that Japanese camp.

The funny little man became a sort of conscience for the camp, its critic, and its standard, and a mirror in which the prisoners saw themselves and how they were behaving.

There was a Christian who did not fail to let his light shine in a truly dark place, and saved himself and others from going to pieces. It is all part of what Jesus meant when he said, 'Let your light so shine before men, that they may see your good works and glorify your Father . . .'

17 A Brave Lad

The young Prince climbed rather wearily up the steep hillside toward a narrow, rocky pass between two great crags. Sometimes he had to use his hands as well as his feet to make any progress up the stiff slope, but the overhanging rocks hid him from the enemy on the other side of the hill, so he climbed safely to the top. With him was a still younger man, really only a lad, charged to carry his master's weapons and armour.

Things were not going well for the king, the Prince's father. His little army, of only six hundred men, was short of weapons. The enemy had taken prisoner all the men who could make helmets and spears, shields, the great metal breast-plates that covered the chest, and the short strong swords needed for hand-to-hand fighting. The Prince, of course, was allowed some of the scarce armour, and a sword: and because he was a Prince, and the stuff was heavy, he was allowed a servant to bear them after him.

That climb up the hill towards the enemy by just the two young men was a daring raid. All round King Saul's little camp the Philistines had set outposts and watchmen to report any attack, or flight; with so many more soldiers, better prepared and armed, and excellent fighters, the Philistines could afford just to wait – to sit it out until King Saul had to give in for lack of food and water.

But Prince Jonathan had other ideas. It might not be very wise to raid the enemy camp on the hill, but it was a brave and brilliant try, and Jonathan believed in God. So he left the king's camp secretly: he said nothing to his father, took only his servant-lad with him, and stole towards the sentries on the hilltop by a path so steep and unexpected that he guessed it would not be guarded properly.

As they neared the top, and the moment of greatest danger, Jonathan explained to his armour-bearer just what they were going to do. It was to be a sudden, surprise attack: because they were only two, they could move silently, quickly, without warning. 'And', said Jonathan, 'it may be that the Lord will work for us; for it makes no difference to God whether he saves by many or by few – by a large army or by just the two of us.'

Princes, I understand, are supposed to be fearless, and great leaders, and very bold. But I wonder what the armour-bearer really felt about this rather crazy scheme! Whatever he felt, he answered very bravely: 'Do all that you have in mind to do. Look, I am with you, and whatever you think, I think. Go ahead!' He may well have been very frightened, but he was certainly very loyal.

So Jonathan proposed a sign by which they should know what God wanted them to do. 'We will go forward', he said, 'to the head of the pass, where the enemy will be able to see us. Then if they say, "Stand where you are! Wait till we come up to you" we will stand still and see what happens. But if they say, "Come on up to us" then we will know that God has given them into our hands. This will be God's sign to us.'

It is all very well being bold and brave: but it is well also to wait for God's guidance to tell you what to do.

And so they did. But when the Philistines saw them, they burst out laughing, and one of them, who thought himself a great joker, called out 'Look, the Hebrews are coming out of their hiding-holes, like rats looking for food!' There was more laughter at that, and when it died down someone else called out to Jonathan and his servant, 'Come on up to us here, we have something to show you'.

'That's it,' said Jonathan quietly, 'that's God's sign – up we go!' So they climbed again on hands and knees to where the Philistines were camped, and – surprise, surprise! – there were only twenty soldiers there! It was still twenty against two, or ten to one, but with God on their side that did not matter. A short, sharp fight, taking advantage of surprise, and Jonathan and his armour-bearer had scattered the Philistines, who fled.

But that was not all, by a long way. This was only a small group of Philistines, set high up on the hilltop to watch the king's army: not far away was the whole might of the Philistines, camped across the open field. But when they heard from the hill the noise and the shouting, and saw the twenty soldiers scatter and fall, they thought a great army must be coming that way, over the hill, to attack when they were not ready. The whole camp panicked – men running to and fro, each part of the army getting in the way of other parts, the horses frightened, stamping and galloping till the very earth shook, all adding to the panic. The whole multitude of the Philistines was surging this way and that, and in the midst of the confusion King Saul's six hundred attacked from the other side. Soon it was all over: the gallant six hundred chased the Philistines out of the countryside.

'So the Lord delivered Israel that day,' by the bravery of Prince Jonathan and the wonderful loyalty of his young armour-bearer. Of course it makes no difference to God to save by many or by few, or even by two if they are brave and loyal fighters. I like Prince Jonathan, but I like that armour-bearer, too, for saying to the Prince in the moment of decision, the moment of danger: 'Do all that you have in mind to do; whatever you think, I think – Go ahead!' It would have been so easy to give way to his fears, and run away: instead, he stood his ground beside his Prince and Captain. Very often, that is the bravest thing you can do – just stand your ground, refuse to give way.

The great warrior, Paul, once said: 'Be strong . . . that you may be able to *stand*, to *withstand* in the evil day, and having done all, to *stand*. *Stand* therefore . . .' Paul was an experienced soldier of Christ: he knew that sometimes the fiercest fight of all is not to rush into attack, but just to stand your ground for what is right and true and good – whatever it costs. This the armour-bearer seems to have understood: instead of turning to run away, 'Go ahead,' he said, 'I am with you.'

Many centuries afterwards – in fact, when I was quite a boy, we used to sing about that brave young lad. Not, as you might think, about Prince Jonathan, but about his serving boy –

> Only an armour-bearer, firmly I stand,
>   Waiting to follow at the king's command:
> Marching, if 'Onward!' shall the order be,
>   Standing by my Captain, serving faithfully.

66

Only an armour-bearer, now in the field
 Guarding a shining helmet, sword, and shield;
Waiting to hear the thrilling battle-cry
 Ready then to answer, 'Master, here am I!'

 Hear ye the battle-cry
 Forward the call
 See, see the faltering ones,
 Backward they fall:

Surely my Captain may depend on me,
 Though but an armour-bearer I may be:
Surely my Captain may depend on me,
 Though but an armour-bearer I may be!

18 Girded for Battle

Bible pictures, and many church windows, have taught us that eastern clothes in Bible times were not very suitable for great effort, whether for travel, for work, or for fighting. The long robes and shawls and things that nearly everyone wore must have been a great nuisance if you wanted to move quickly, or swing a sword or throw a spear. That is why we read so often the call to 'Gird up your loins' – which means, quite simply, 'Be ready!' 'Tighten your belt!' 'Tie your robes up clear of your knees and make sure they will not slip and trip you up!'

'Stand, therefore, having your loins girt about with truth' says Paul, as though the one thing that made the Christian soldier *ready* always for the good fight of faith, was – to know the truth and be true. Truth is a strong belt, which saves us from being tripped up when we fight for what is right. But why all this talk about *fighting*?

I

William Booth began life very poor, about one hundred and fifty years ago, starting work in a 'shop' which lent money to even poorer people, desperate for food. In that first job William learned all about the lives of people without decent homes, or sufficient food, or any comfort, or love, or hope; all too often their suffering led into degradation, disease, sometimes into drunkenness and sin. And William never forgot.

He began as a young man to preach 'salvation' from all kinds of evil through our Lord Jesus Christ, at first in his spare time, but later, when a business man offered to pay him equal to his wages, William preached and worked for Christ full time. Later still he was made a minister.

But still he could not forget those early days. Soon he chose to leave his comfortable church to preach on street corners, in

rough halls, among the worst slums of east London. He believed passionately that the church of Jesus should be 'militant' – warlike – against all forms of suffering and evil, and should go onto the attack. He faced much ridicule, of course, and criticism, and very soon threats and actual violence from those who did not like his 'interference' with their evil ways, or their wicked profits.

Other people joined William, stirred by his courage, and the 'mission' grew. But so did the opposition, and the sharpness of the constant battle against poverty, drunkenness, vice, and misery. Out of all this came that strange name for a *Christian* organisation, 'the Salvation Army', with its military-sounding bands, its flags, its street marches and parades, its uniforms, and its ministers with military titles like Captain, Major, and the rest. William himself soon became known everywhere as 'General' Booth. It all made quite clear to everyone what a fierce fight was being undertaken.

Very quickly the work of the 'Army' came to include providing cheap lodging and food for the poor, training in work, and all kinds of help for anyone in need. In spite of this, opposition increased. The bands' instruments were stolen, or snatched from players and destroyed; the torn 'skins' of expensive drums were exhibited as trophies in drinking-houses; young women in uniform were attacked, and preachers stoned in the streets; preaching-halls were ransacked and burned down. Those who made rich profits from selling alcohol, from vice and poor housing, from other people's weaknesses, poverty and misery, were cruel and ruthless in trying to prevent any improvement, help, education or reform.

But 'General' Booth was equally determined to continue the fight, and steadily gathered thousands of helpers. He 'laid down his sword' and died in 1912, at eighty-two years of age, still very eager for battle. By that time he had written a very powerful book exposing the evils he fought against. He was an honoured 'Freeman' of the city of Nottingham (his birthplace), and also of the city of London. He had been received – in full Salvation Army uniform – by the King. But he was still fighting – he never compromised to win favour.

At a great Rally in the Albert Hall in London, just before he died, William made his last speech in public, and the very last sentences were: 'While women weep, as they do now, I'll fight; while little children go hungry, as they do now; I'll fight; while men go to prison, in and out, in and out, as they do now, I'll fight; while there is a drunkard left, while there is a poor lost girl upon the streets, while there remains one dark soul without the light of God, I'll fight – I'll fight to the very end.'

There was a man girded for battle in the good fight of faith.

II

Charles Péan was a little man, like Paul, and a Salvation Army officer in France. Though gentle and mild in manner, he was stubborn, and had tremendous courage. It was the Salvation Army's motto in France – 'A man may be down, but he is never out' – which fired Charles' zeal; and a newspaper's exposure of the appalling conditions in France's special colony for punishing hardened criminals, which challenged Charles' courage.

This colony was called 'Devil's Island'. All France was shocked at repeated reports of the brutality, sickness, viciousness, and violence, the degradation and hopelessness of men, on this dreadful island-prison. More than seventy thousand had died there. Many had been driven mad, or had caught terrible diseases and received no care or treatment. Some were chained, some starved to death. And it was almost impossible for a man ever to get free, even when his sentence was completed. While many were shocked at it all, Charles Péan simply felt sickened by what he heard – and determined that something must be done.

After months spent pestering the Prison Authorities and the government, Charles Péan visited Devil's Island, investigated things for himself, and blazed with anger and disgust. For the prisoners he felt deeply sorry; what made him angry was the resistance of officials anxious to let well alone; and the helpless despair of a few who agreed that reform was badly needed, but who said 'This is a little hell which no man can conquer: perhaps it's even too big for God!' 'That', said Charles, 'remains to be seen.'

On returning to France, Charles was struck down for

eighteen months with tropical fever caught on the visit – surely excuse enough to leave Devil's Island alone and keep far away. But not for Charles. As he slowly recovered he made his plans: ultimately, he would get the prison settlement abolished altogether; meanwhile, as a first step, he would reform it. As soon as he was able, he began his campaign, writing, preaching, travelling, interviewing officials, always exposing and condemning what he had seen. In the end, the French Ministry of Justice agreed to let him return to the Island, with three other Salvation Army officers, to try to improve things. At least that would get rid of him from France!

The whole task was daunting – even frightening. They were not welcomed. Their possessions were stolen. Their first attempts were deliberately frustrated by officials on the spot, who then reported back to France their failures. Their plans were ridiculed, and the prisoners they persuaded to co-operate with them merely got drunk and violent. Traps were set to catch out those who tried to help them; lies were sent back home to discredit their work; their money and accounts were deliberately falsified to make them appear thieves – a hundred difficulties and forms of opposition were invented. But Charles was stubborn. *He* could fight too!

A reasonable home, for those whose sentences were finished; a farm to provide work, and better food; workshops for furniture and carving to be sold for wages; a banana plantation; and the possibility of saving up, and returning home to France as new men – all were created by Charles Péan's sheer stubbornness and courage. Whatever happened, whatever was contrived against him, however people let him down, he would not give up. He *fought*, against the evil in men, against the laziness or dishonesty of officials, against the unwillingness of distant authorities – he *fought*, with the help of Salvationists and others who came to believe in his plan.

And while he fought, Péan was also teaching his terrible congregation of criminals the love and forgiveness of Christ. By the time war interrupted his work, he had sent home as freed and trained men, eight hundred and four of the convicts. And when the war ended, France immediately decided to close down Devil's Island for good – and appointed Charles Péan to carry out the order.

Returning, on Good Friday, to the Island for the last time, Charles Péan was greeted with a pathway of *flowers*. On Easter Day, at a great gathering of those whom Péan had served for eighteen years, he wore on his uniform the ribbon of France's highest reward, the Legion of Honour. But when his turn came, he could not speak for tears – tears of joy.

Another bonny fighter, girded for battle in the good fight of faith.

19 Pirates, Pigs and Poetry

No one is sure where Succat came from. Most probably it was
from the banks of the Clyde River, in Scotland, possibly
where Dumbarton Rock still rears its massive bulk above the
water beside Kirk Patrick (as it is called today, Kilpatrick).
Succat's family were Christians, leaders in the little wooden
church beside the river, but the boy himself made little of
Christian teaching. Because his father was a farmer, Succat
spent most of his earliest years looking after sheep, and on the
whole his life was peaceful and pleasant – even dull. Except
when the warning sped along the river bank –'PIRATES!'

The pirates came rowing silently up the wide mouth of the
Clyde from Ireland, raiding the shore farms for cattle, and
when they could catch them, for people. About the year 405,
when Succat was sixteen or so, a large pirate band 'invaded'
the district, and a number of people were caught unprepared,
captured, and carried off. They included Succat and his two
sisters: and all were taken to be sold as slaves in Ireland.

Lonely, homesick, and afraid, Succat suddenly found that
his family's religion *did* mean something. 'Day by day as I
went, a shepherd, with my flock, I used to pray constantly, a
hundred prayers, and as many in the night again,' Succat
wrote later on. Some versions of the story say that in Ireland
he kept pigs, not sheep.

Six years went by before Succat had opportunity to escape.
Then, a two-hundred-miles tramp brought him to the seashore, where he begged for work on a ship, hoping to return
to Scotland. But the ship took him instead to France.

Here, after other adventures, including almost starving to
death, Succat met again people like his family and friends at
home, Christians who cared for him, and monks who served
God among the poor. Because of the way God had heard and
answered his prayers, Succat felt bound to offer himself for
God's service, and after training and discipline he too became

a monk. It was at this time that Succat was given the new Christian name which everybody knows – *Patrick* (remember – Kirk *Patrick*?)

His training finished, Patrick longed to return home, and what a welcome he was given at the farm by the river! He was now a grown man, ready to take the lead in the family, and in the little church. 'They received me as a son,' he wrote, 'and besought me after all I had been through not to leave them to go anywhere at all.' We might think he would not need much persuasion to stay put.

But Patrick was too eager and too energetic to settle down. Memories of Ireland, and of its people, and of other slaves far from their homes, kept disturbing his sleep. He dreamt once of a man from Ireland bringing him letters, and a call from those he had known there to 'return, and walk among us once more'. Like Paul, dreaming of the man from Macedonia saying 'Come over and help us', Patrick too felt that *God* was calling him to return to Ireland. Indeed, Patrick came to see that God had led him through all this trouble, through capture, and homesickness, and slavery, and to France, just to prepare him to go back to Ireland with Christ's message. Instead of wanting to return for revenge, Patrick planned to return in love.

Gathering some helpers, (and some say, taking more training, too), Patrick set out for Ireland. Strange to say, when they landed they in turn were mistaken for pirates, and the local people prepared to defend themselves. Patrick walked forward, unarmed, and spoke so quietly and gently that he was soon welcomed as a friend, and with his men taken to the house of the local leading man for a feast. But Patrick would not eat until he had told his message of God's love. Very soon, his friendliness won support; a huge barn was cleared for a church, and Patrick's Christian mission to Ireland had begun.

Yet it was not Patrick's friendliness alone that won success, but also his fearlessness. Most of Ireland still followed the ancient Druid religion, and the Druid leaders were very jealous of their power and antagonistic to the new faith. Each springtime, a great Druid festival was held at Tara, where the king of Ireland lived with his court. For the festival, by the order of the Druids, the whole countryside was kept in darkness, all fires and lights forbidden on pain of death, until the chief Druid should light fire on the heathen altar to show that the warm sun was returning.

Suddenly, one year, while the country people shivered with cold and fear because of the vast darkness, a great blaze sprang up not far from the court, shedding bright light on the surrounding hills and offering warmth and gladness again. The Druid leaders were exceedingly angry, and urged the king to send men to arrest and punish whoever was responsible. They came, and found Patrick, and he was ordered to be seized and brought before the king: but Patrick cried out 'Let God arise!' – and no one dared to touch him.

Instead, Patrick walked with the men, quietly, leaving his weapons behind, and came towards the king, looking dignified, unafraid, confident. When the king demanded of him 'Who are you?' Patrick answered, 'I am a torch-bearer: I bring the true light to lighten this dark land, and to spread peace and goodwill.' Attracted and impressed by Patrick's courage, the king listened, and asked to be told more. Eventually he gave permission for the people to be taught of this new light and love of the Christian gospel.

The Druids of course were resentful, and did not give in. Many attempts were made to murder Patrick, but always he seemed to be protected, and escaped. Rumours began to spread that he wore a magic armour. In fact, Patrick and his men wore long sheepskin cloaks, and carried leather satchels with copies of the Gospels, and a bell to call each town or village to hear their message. Their only armour was their good purpose, to make known the love of God and what was right in God's sight – what Paul calls 'the breastplate of righteousness'.

Thrice armed is he who hath his quarrel *just* . . . only Patrick had no quarrel, except with those who wished to keep the gospel from the common people.

Gradually, little wooden churches like the one Patrick loved in Scotland, began to spring up in many places, and to the end of his life Patrick preached, organised, wrote poems, and composed songs, meeting all opposition with friendliness, fearlessness, and unfailing good temper – 'a brave and lovable man'.

That rumour about Patrick's magic armour may however explain why a famous poem (which many would still say Patrick himself wrote) is always called 'St Patrick's Breastplate'. Part of it says –

> I bind unto myself today
>   The power of God to hold and lead,
> His eye to watch, his might to stay,
>   His ear to hearken to my need,
> The wisdom of my God to teach,
>   His hand to guide, his shield to ward,
> The word of God to give me speech,
>   His heavenly host to be my guard.
>
> Christ be with me, Christ within me,
>   Christ behind me, Christ before me,
> Christ beside me, Christ to win me,
>   Christ to comfort and restore me;
> Christ beneath me, Christ above me,
>   Christ in quiet, Christ in danger,
> Christ in hearts of all that love me,
>   Christ in mouth of friend and stranger . . .

but there is much more. Whoever first wrote the words, they make a fine, strong 'breastplate' to guard a friendly and fearless heart!

20 Stolen Shoes

My sister and I had one favourite walk for all school holidays; year after year we would go the same way and explore the same places. It seemed a long walk when we were young – about three miles each way – and I am afraid that *one* reason why we liked it was that we could leave our little brother at home. It was too far for him.

But there were less selfish reasons, too. The road ran high above a winding river, which it was exciting to look down upon as it flowed between spreading fields and little woods. Then, there was a racecourse near the river, and we always hoped to see the horses running, though we never seemed to plan the right day, except once. At the end of the walk a pretty little stone bridge crossed the river into a small village – a truly wonderful place.

Caerleon-upon-Usk, so we believed, had once been the court of the great King Arthur and his famous Knights of the Round Table. Even before that, it had been the headquarters of a Roman army when the Romans conquered Britain and held Caerleon as a river-fort against the fierce Welsh raiders.

So, of course, the village had its little museum, with bits of Roman pottery (which did not interest us very much), and tiles from Roman houses, and many, many Roman coins. The Romans seem to have been exceptionally clumsy with their crockery, and exceedingly careless with their cash! And across the road from the museum was – the 'amphitheatre', or arena.

It looked, as I remember it now, rather like a small football ground, with a level green oval surrounded by a grassy bank where ages ago the spectators sat and watched whatever was going on. In those days the centre oval would not be green, but rough stones and sand: and the games would not be football or gymnastics, but fierce fights in which men died, sometimes in horrible ways. Captured British prisoners would often be forced to fight with trained Roman soldiers until they could fight no more, and were beheaded. Sometimes they fought with animals: wolves as we were told, and even bears. And occasionally Romans would fight each other, for rich prizes and great fame, and wrestlers would do so too – all to provide amusement for an idle afternoon. My sister and I used to wander round this place, looking for coins, or trying to imagine the soldiers in their armour, the chariots and horses, the Roman ladies – and the wolves!

One summer afternoon there was great excitement, and a lot of people were milling around. We could not understand what was going on. We asked, of course, but we were pushed away in the rude way grown-ups have. Meanwhile, everybody went on talking in little groups about – 'the find'.

What had been found? You will never, never guess. We did not find out, until a newspaper told the story. Someone had found, in the Roman arena at Caerleon, a prayer.

Yes, that's right a *prayer*. And such a prayer, too.

At the entrance to the amphitheatre was a little square of stones set into the ground. These were all that were left of the foundation of a small room that had once stood by the arena gate. This room, so we now learned, had been a tiny temple to a Roman goddess, probably Minerva. There, Romans ordered to fight in the arena would offer prayer for courage and victory, or for a swift death. Their prayers were written by a priest, backwards for secrecy, on lead tablets, folded and laid at the feet of the idol-goddess. It was of no use to speak to an idol, of course – but they seem to have thought that she could read – and backwards!

One of these tablets had just been found, after over fifteen hundred years. No wonder people were excited. But what a very strange, dreadful, spiteful prayer it was: 'Cursed be the man who stole my shoes!'

'*Cursed be the man who stole my shoes!*' Yes, prayers can be spiteful, and selfish, full of envy sometimes, and of anger. Some Roman, long long ago, had asked the goddess to take revenge on whoever had stolen his fighting shoes.

You can guess why. Suppose that you had no other shoes, but only one pair; or suppose your second-best pair was worn, the straps ready to break. It could be very dangerous to slip on the sandy ground just as a bear rushed at you and you tried to streak away – or to feel a sharp stone cut your heel just as you dodged the leap of an angry wolf. It could mean death, to feel a strap break and your ankle twist, just as a sword thrust made you dart aside.

Someone had stolen a gladiator's shoes, to make it almost certain he would be killed. That is why the angry soldier, or slave, had gone to the temple, had his prayer inscribed, paid his fee to the priest, and left his bitter request at the feet of the goddess.

I wonder if he was killed, or lived to fight again?

It was many years after that summer visit that I noticed what the Bible says about the Christian armed to fight with evil with a helmet and a breastplate and a sword and a shield, and 'your feet shod with the readiness of the gospel' – and I remembered that prayer. How can you fight, or even stand firm, in bare feet?

No one can fight while he is slipping and slithering about on rough, or even on slippery, ground. You must first get a firm foothold. Certainly you cannot fight for anything good, or against anything evil, until you know where you stand, and what you stand for – *and stand there.* You will never resist bad things unless you plant your feet firmly on what is good, and refuse to be pushed around.

Weak, uncertain, undecided people, when they go wrong, usually complain that it was only a slip – or that someone swept them off their feet. A wise man once answered, 'It is always a question of where your feet were, before you slipped!' That is what Paul was thinking of, as he urged his young Christian friends to put on the gospel shoes and 'Stand up, stand up for Jesus!'

Let no one steal *your* fighting shoes, whatever you do.

21 Shielded by Faith

Mary stood on the pavement, scornfully confronting a boy who had been bullying smaller children in a particularly stupid way. He had tied a piece of lead to a length of string, and was swinging it round his head – a very dangerous thing to do, for if the string snapped or slipped from his hold it could hurt someone badly.

Mary had found him threatening the children with this silly 'toy', and though she was small, and only fifteen, she rushed in to stop him. Angrily he faced her, and swung his lead faster, edging towards her to drive her away. But Mary never would be driven, not by *anyone* – much less a silly lout of a boy! She stood her ground, the lead swinging nearer and nearer to her face, until it just scraped her brow and drew blood. Then, frightened at what he had done, the coward swore at her and ran away – beaten by a slim girl's stout courage.

Years later, Mary was in one of the wildest and most dangerous places in the world, on the west coast of Africa, a place of fevers, disease, and poisonous swamps, of jungle animals and snakes, of fierce warring tribes, wandering gangs of murderers and thieves, of savage customs, of revenge demanded on somebody – no matter who – for every illness, accident, or death. Men there took intense pride in the number of people they had killed: so that to show a man's importance when he died, all his children, his wives, and his servants, were killed too. Children, and women, suffered appallingly; unwanted or sickly children (especially twins) were simply left for animals or ants to eat, whenever their fathers were tired of them.

To that dreaded 'slum of Africa', Mary had chosen to go to teach the way of Christ. 'Because', she said, 'the post of danger is the post of honour.'

She loved to pioneer new places, often going where men were afraid to go. Once, when the men refused to go forward into the forest by night, Mary set off to keep a promise, with five children she had rescued from death, a boy of eleven tired and afraid, another of eight in tears, another of three howling, a girl of five sobbing with fear, and a baby girl on her shoulders. She herself was inwardly afraid, too: but kept singing nonsense for the children's sake, tramping four miles, getting the children safely into bed, and then returning four miles for the men and the food! What hope had a bullying coward against a character like that?

Another time, a drunken man approached her house carrying his gun, which was forbidden. Mary commanded him to place it in a corner, but he refused. She strode forward and simply took it out of his hands, stood it there herself, and forbade him to touch it for a week. He obeyed. Mary, long before, had had too much to do with her own drunken father, walking the streets at night with smaller children to keep them out of his way, to have much patience or fear towards drunken men.

A village chief was very ill, and Mary was sent for: but the chief of her own village advised her not to go. He pointed out that if the sick man died, there would be killings and revenge, and she would be in danger. Besides, he added, after eight hours of rain the streams were swollen and the paths deep in mud. Mary thought of the wives and children in fear of being killed, and she set out. It took three hours, and she arrived muddy, soaked, weary, and exhausted, and fearing that because of this she would be despised. In fact, the villagers were amazed that a *woman* could show such determination. From that time the district was open to her as 'a Great Woman'.

Two years later came news of a fatal accident, followed by the usual killing for 'revenge'. But the man so killed was a village chief, and his death meant war. Again Mary set out, everyone advising her it was too late, for the warriors had drunk much wine and the war drums were already sounding. Mary agreed to call on a friendly chief for escort – but he avoided helping, wanting to keep out of trouble. He said that the tribe concerned were a war-loving people, not likely to be helped by a woman. Mary replied curtly, 'In measuring the woman's power you have evidently forgotten to take into account the woman's God!'

Pressing onwards, in double danger now from the excited warriors and from the offended chief, Mary was suddenly surrounded and fiercely questioned. By bold and skilful replies, she obtained a promise of no fighting until she had heard the whole story. For all that, the younger fighters, out of their elders' control, and yelling the war cries, were off at daybreak for a great killing. But Mary caught up with them, and angrily told them to behave like men, and not like fools!

Then she strode straight on to the enemy village, to be greeted by a sullen silence: so she complimented them on their perfect manners. As she tried to pass through the line of armed men to approach their leader, an old man stepped forward and knelt before her, pleading that she should make the avenging soldiers understand that it was all one man's fault. This was the old chief whose life she had saved ten years before. At once Mary ordered both sides to provide her with food and to find her a comfortable seat for a 'palaver'. She ordered that two from each side should argue the case before her – knowing that this, too, would take time.

Following a long meal, and after hours and hours of talk, the payment of a fine was arranged, and because this would lead at once to great drunkenness, Mary stayed on to control the party, throwing some of her clothes over the stores of wine: no one would dare to touch it, then, until she gave permission. In that way, with talk, and singing, and endless laughter, Mary kept them all in good humour 'till the morning. Then when all were tired out, she preached to both sides until they promised solemnly not to fight while she went on holiday.

When such palavers went on all the day and half the night, Mary would spend the time knitting, quietly listening, distracting the bewildered villagers by her remarks on her changes of knitting-pattern, and often intervening in the argument with great fun. Another trick, to give herself time to reach some quarrelling tribe threatening bloodshed, was to scrawl huge and imposing marks all over a large sheet of paper, drop sealing wax all round it, and send it forward to be read carefully by both sides before the fighting started. While they were still puzzling out what this important 'document' might mean, Mary would arrive.

Another time, although terrified of snakes and leopards, she lay all night on the path in the forest, between two quarrelling groups, determined not to move until the men – who would not dare to pass her – gave up and went home.

Dozens of such stories – all true stories, too – can be told about the indomitable Scots girl from Dundee. Poor, uneducated, with a sorry home background, out to work at eleven years of age, and with very few advantages, she came to be revered as Queen of Calabar. For forty years she lived in that most perilous part of Africa among a violent people, teaching, laughing, singing, scolding, pleading, outwitting them, dosing them, sometimes boxing their ears, rescuing children, serving everyone in every possible way, in the name of Jesus.

Her own village chief came publicly to say 'Thank you', and stayed on privately to kneel before her, holding her feet, and saying: 'We are all weary of the old customs, but none of us has power to break with them.' One by one others came to urge her to keep on, saying that in their hearts they knew that she was right and the Christian way best. Mary Slessor died in 1915 – and in our own time, a noble Queen has stood with head bowed at her grave in Calabar.

The only explanation of such a character, such astonishing courage, such achievement, lies in her own words to that reluctant chief: 'in measuring the woman's power you evidently have forgotten to take into account the woman's God'. There speaks Mary's inmost heart. She trusted at all times, implicitly, even when she was afraid – and especially when she was afraid – *in God*. Day in, day out, and through the night as well, she carried the 'shield of faith', which the apostle Paul urged all Christians to carry, to quench the fiery darts of every kind of evil.

It's a good tip.

22 Mind Your Head!

> Prepare buckler and shield,
>> and advance for battle!
> Harness the horses –
>> mount, O horsemen!
> Take your stations with your helmets,
>> polish your spears,
>> put on your coats of mail!

The prophet Jeremiah is calling to Egypt's army to prepare for war, and what a stirring picture he paints – the shining shields, small round ones (bucklers) for the foot-soldiers and large ones for the horsemen; the jingling, polished harness and the glossy horses; spears bright in the sun and held at a slant, flashing back the light like a row of mirrors; the commanders probably distinguished by shoulder-pieces like sleeves, and skirts over their thighs, made up of bronze discs linked together – 'coats of mail' gleaming and sounding one against the other quietly as the horses stirred.

Noblest item of all in the imposing array would be the lines of glistening helmets of the special men, the officers and the leaders of battle. Those helmets were most likely of burnished bronze, built high over the head with a ridge or band of brass running from front to back, and with 'cheek-pieces' to shield the face and a metal guard curving downwards over the back of the neck: thus they completely guarded the head from sword thrust, from battle-axe and flying arrows. In our day, oil-rig men and miners, and building-site workers, wear very plain helmets to guard against falling tools or stones. We may laugh at 'tin hats', but they are very necessary.

A few years ago firemen used to wear helmets not unlike those of the Egyptian army – gorgeous brass ones with metal badges and straps or chains under their chins. These too, were essential to protect the brave men from falling timbers and

walls in their dangerous work: but how grand they looked! Small boys, at any rate, thought very little of the crowns worn by kings and queens, compared with the shining helmet of a real fireman! Goliath, the giant of Gath, whom David fought, had just such a helmet of brass: it must have added inches to his height, and fierceness to his frightening look.

But in olden days the officers's helmets had even more than bright metal and badges to make them conspicuous and glorious: to each was fixed a high plume, of eagles' feathers or flowing silken strands, or dyed fur, or some such thing. By that brightly coloured plume, the ordinary soldier in the thick of the fight would know his own leader and rally to him, and keep close beside him. In this way, recognition depended on the helmet, as well as protection, and encouragement, too: for so long as the Commander bravely rode his horse, his plume tossing above the battle, men took heart from his courage and fought on. And when a warrior died, his shield, and his helmet with his own distinctive plume, was often hung above his house, or over his grave, or in some temple, in memory of him.

Remembering all this, we must feel very sorry for Don Quixote. According to the famous Spanish story, Don Quixote was at the start a simple gentleman, who read many books of poetry and tales of famous knights who wandered here and there through the wide world doing brave deeds, putting wrongs right, defending the oppressed, and – especially – rescuing lovely ladies from cruel fathers or wicked rulers or unworthy would-be-husbands. The tale tells that so much reading turned his brain a little mad, and he set out fired with a burning zeal to imitate the things of which his head was full.

Unfortunately, his imagination led him sadly astray. He saw everyone, everything, ordinary and simple people and things, as though they all belonged to these romantic poems and stories – a little wayside inn appeared to him a great Spanish castle; two country serving girls he imagined to be two great noblewomen, so that he gave them high-sounding titles – Lady This, and the Duchess of That. His bony, half-starved, stumbling horse, he said, was the finest steed in the world. He mistook a group of merchants, who were travelling to buy silk, for a gang of fierce brigands out to waylay him; and thirty or forty windmills, whose sails moved slowly in the breeze, he attacked as mighty giants wielding four arms each!

Setting out on his well-meant but very muddled adventures, Quixote first cleaned up some old armour which had belonged to his ancestors but which now lay rusted, the leather straps green with mould. He repaired and polished as well as he could, but the helmet was incomplete. The visor – a hinged piece that should cover the upper part of his face – was missing, leaving him in serious danger of a wound to his eyes or his forehead. So Quixote made a *cardboard* visor to look as nearly like the real thing as he could manage, and fastened it in place. Then he tested it: he brought his sword down hard across the helmet, and the visor of course shattered into pieces.

Angry, Quixote made another; but this time he fastened pieces of iron underneath the cardboard: and this time he would not test it – in case it broke again!

So he went out on his adventures. At an inn where he stayed for the night, though he was hungry and weary he would not let anyone remove his helmet. The maids could not untie the ribbon-knots which held it on, and Quixote would not have the ribbons cut lest the helmet come to pieces. So he

had to be fed through the visor – bits of bread pushed between the strips of iron and wine poured through a reed
between his lips! And after some fashion he slept – with his
helmet on.

In his first quarrel, Quixote was beaten with the wooden
pieces of his own lance, and his helmet failed to protect his head
at all. In his first real fight, he rashly challenged a strong man,
well-armed, and only just escaped. As it was, his enemy's heavy
sword caught Quixote beside the head, the visor simply fell off,
the metal split, and Quixote lost an ear . . . And so the story goes
on and on, for fifty or more adventures altogether, all foolish,
crazy, ill-managed, perilous. But nothing Quixote ever did was
more perilous, more stupid, than setting out to do battle against
wrong with his *head* unprotected.

That is what Paul had in mind when he urged us to 'put on
the helmet of salvation' – to let Christ save our heads, guarding well our *minds*, and our *imagination* – the things we picture to our secret selves; bringing every *thought* under his
control; setting a watch upon our eyes and the way we look at
things, and upon our lips and everything we say. For our head
is the ruling part of us: if that is safe in Christ's directing
hands – all may be well with us.

Bravery is fine – but not enough. Skill is good – but not
enough. Brave and skilful fighters must never lose their heads.
That is why what is known as the Knights' Prayer, written in
the sixteenth century, and perhaps at first in French in the
fifteenth century, pleads –

> God be in my head,
>   And in my understanding;
> God be in mine eyes,
>   And in my looking;
> God be in my mouth,
>   And in my speaking;
> God be in my heart,
>   And in my thinking;
> God be at mine end,
>   And at my departing.

A helmet for the cleverest head!

23 Sword Play

Some stories get told so often down the generations from
fathers to children or from grandfathers to grand-daughters
that no one can remember if they are really true, or mainly
true with imaginary bits, or entirely made-up. Things get
added, or left out, each time a tale is told, and sometimes the
story grows differently in different places. The stories about
King Arthur are like that: magic, fairy story, and history of
ancient Britain and France, are all mixed up.

But one thing in all the stories of King Arthur gleams and
flashes again and again – King Arthur's sword. That he once
ruled parts of Britain, fought the Saxon invaders, gathered a
wonderful 'Round Table' of noble knights to share his stirring
adventures and fine deeds: this much *may* be true. And that
Arthur himself was a splendid soldier, a fine swordsman, and
a good king.

One story says that when he was a baby, Arthur was
wickedly taken from his parents and brought up by someone
else: who he really was – the son of King Uther Pendragon,
and heir to his father's throne – was only discovered long
afterwards, by a very strange circumstance. Somewhere in
London, outside an ancient church, stood a great iron anvil,
such as smiths use to make horseshoes on. But straight
through *this* anvil (so the story says) was thrust a splendid
sword. No one could draw it out except the future King of
England. Arthur's older cousin once left his sword accidentally at an inn, and young Arthur was sent back to find it. But
the inn was locked up and deserted. Passing the ancient
church, Arthur in curiosity laid his hand upon the hilt of the
splendid anvil-sword – and it came out easily.

Only some say it was not an anvil at all, but a great stone,
that had the sword fastened through it; and say it all happened
somewhere else.

Again, some versions of the story say that *that* sword was

the mighty Excalibur, which Arthur wielded in great battles all his life, and which marvellously protected him in all dangers and won him endless victories. But then again, others say that Excalibur was given to Arthur when the first sword broke, by a lovely and mysterious 'Lady of the Lake'. She appeared when Arthur was weary and disarmed after a great battle, and showed him a new sword, gem-studded and bright and sharp, held high above the water of a lake, as though by someone beneath the surface – only a white arm, clothed in fine silk, and the hand grasping the hilt, were visible.

Arthur longed to possess that sword, and asked how he might win it. He was told simply to row out upon the water and to take it. For the rest of his life, Arthur fought, and ruled, and enforced justice, defended the weak, rescued captives, and much else, by the power of Excalibur. It is said that the strange name means 'cut-steel'. When Arthur was finally wounded in battle, a barge appeared upon the same lake to

bear him away for healing, or to die (the story-tellers are not sure which). But before he left, Excalibur was thrown, by one of his knights, spinning through the air, flashing in the sunlight, across the same water, and once again the arm appeared above the surface, clothed in white, to catch the hilt, brandish the sword three times, and withdraw it beneath the waters 'until Arthur shall need it again'.

Well, it's a fine old tale, even if it is fanciful. And here is an older one, similar but true, to set beside it. Centuries before King Arthur, in ancient Israel, young David fled for his life with a few friends, out of reach of the anger of King Saul. Hungry and weary, he came to the house of God at Nob, to beg for bread. He pleaded also for arms, because in his haste he had left his spear and sword at home. The priest at Nob was at first afraid to help David, but he relented, and gave him some of the holy bread set out in the temple before God. As for arms, he had none to offer, except (would you believe it?) the great sword of the giant Goliath, whom David himself had killed.

It seems that that mighty sword – a Hebrew 'Excalibur' – had been carefully wrapped in cloth to keep it sharp and bright, and laid behind God's altar, a sacred memorial and thanksgiving for David's mighty exploit when Israel was in peril from the Philistines. No one else could use that heavy weapon, but now the priest brought it out and offered it to David, who surely had won the right, more than any other man, to use and to possess it. So the sword of Goliath became in later years King David's sword, and went with him through all his royal battles and his great conquests.

But enough of sword-play. It is rather grim, and terrible, when you really think about it. What really matters is, that here are two ancient stories full of a sense that everything fine and lovely, everything right and pure, everything true and godly, *has to be fought for* in this world. And full, too, of the thought that if a man is to fight well he must go armed with a worthy weapon and the strength to use it.

As we grow older we come to realise that some of the hardest fighting of all is not with swords and spears, nor yet with guns and planes, but against temptation and the pressure to do wrong. The Bible so often warns us of the evil that is around us, and within our own hearts, and calls us to watch, be alert, and go armed, not only with helmet, breastplate, shield and shoes, but with the sword of the Spirit, which is the word of God. That is not hard to understand, if we remember how Jesus faced temptation in the wilderness, answering each evil suggestion with the very words of God quoted from the scriptures. That's good sword play! If Jesus needed the sword of God's word, needed to know and understand and use the scripture, in his fight for God, how much more do we. To know the Bible well, and to learn by practice how to wield its wonderful stories, and examples, and its advice and promises, against all the arguments of evil, is to carry a sword sharper than Excalibur, and go better armed even than Goliath.

> What evil fate soever
> For me remains in store,
> 'Tis sure much finer fellows
> Have faced much worse before.
>
> So here are things to think on
> That ought to make me brave,
> As I strap on for fighting
> My sword . . .

the word of God.

24 In Touch with HQ

Being a Christian in the first century was certainly no easier than being a Christian in our own time. That is why Paul was so anxious that his young converts should be ready to stand firm and fight bravely for their faith in Christ.

And that is why he urges them to put on the whole armour of God – to gird their loins for battle lest they be tripped up; to strap the strong breastplate of right living about their heart; to take good care that their feet are shod with the readiness which a clear decision for Christ confers; to carry always the shield of faith to ward off fears and perils; to guard their minds with the helmet of salvation, and have always near to hand the spiritual sword of the word of God.

Such armour offers secure and complete coverage – except for your back! But the true Christian never turns his back upon the enemy.

One might think that, so armed, the Christian was ready for anything. Yet one important thing is missing. A man may be well harnessed with all protection and good weapons, and a brave fighter into the bargain, and yet be picked off by the enemy quite easily if he wanders about the battlefield on his own, or faces in the wrong direction, or gets lost in the fray until he hardly knows which side he is on. A soldier must be disciplined, always under command, waiting for directions, ready to obey orders. He cannot hope to see the whole fight from where he stands: only the Captain, and beyond him the General, understands how the battle is going. The ordinary, individual soldier has somehow to keep in touch. It could make all the difference to his own safety, to the safety of his comrades, and even to the outcome of the fight.

Many clever ways have been used to keep fighting men in touch with their Headquarters. Perhaps the oldest of all were the standards, the banners and flags, and the helmet-plumes, raised over the battlefield to show each man where he should keep close and in which direction his Commander was moving. Strong, swift young men were usually appointed standard-bearers, under orders to keep the flag flying at all costs, to keep the army together. Ships' flags, with their clever messages to distant ships or to the shore, are similar 'speaking banners', and they are still used for some communications, even in these days of radio. Everyone remembers how Nelson's famous flag-signal put new heart into all his fighting men – 'England expects that every man will do his duty'.

'Heliograph' was a way of sending messages by mirrors, reflecting long or short or varying flashes of sunlight over great distances, and spelling out (if you were clever enough to read them) important commands. Rather similar was the 'semaphore' method, by which a man's arms waving about his head spelled out letters that made up messages. One danger was that the enemy might read them, and another was that the sender – who had to be clearly seen – might be attacked. So, sometimes, a mechanical 'semaphore' was used instead.

Pigeons were often employed to send war news, and even commands, over long distances, the messages being sealed in small tubes strapped to the pigeon's leg. Probably the champion of these brave and miraculously clever birds was one owned by the famous fighting Duke of Wellington: released with an important despatch from a ship off the West Coast of Africa, it made the longest known homing-flight to England in fifty-five days. The poor bird just made it, and dropped dead one mile from its home-loft, after about seven thousand miles.

With the invention of the electric telegraph, keeping in touch with Army Headquarters became much easier, as messages could be tapped out in dots and dashes, 'the Morse code'. Brave men of the Royal Corps of Signals had first to lay the miles of wire, often through fields and woods where fighting continued around them. One very famous story of the first 'World War' told of a young signaller who lay wounded in mud, desperately holding together with his bare hands the two ends of a broken wire, that the message might get through.

Then, of course, radio made it possible to dispense with wires and talk with 'HQ' through the air. Again the enemy could listen, so many ingenious ways were practised of getting your meaning through while baffling those who 'listened in'. Complicated codes were invented in the hope that no one without the key would be able to decipher the message – though equally brilliant people often discovered the key for themselves and gained valuable information. Two or three officers in the Far East managed to hide their talk to each other in figures, which only they themselves knew were book, chapter, and verse in the Bible. Two or three others spoke quite freely on the radio about important things affecting warfare in the jungle: but they spoke in Welsh!

All of which illustrates how important it is for fighting men to keep in touch with their commanders. Paul was thinking of the Christian's earnest fight for truth and right, when he urged the young Christians at Ephesus not only to go armed for battle but to 'pray at all times, with all prayer and supplication; to that end keep alert with all perseverance, making supplication . . .' That is, when you are fully armed, do not forget, for a moment, to keep in touch with your Commander: know how, and where, and when, he would have you fight.

So to the story: it was during the second World War, and at the end of a daring raid by small ships on the occupied coast of France. As the little boats turned homewards, a Canadian minister – the 'padre' to the fighting men – saw some men left behind among the cliffs and caves. Turning to the men around him in the boat he asked why they had been left behind, to be found by the enemy. They replied that the men were wounded, and could not be carried back in time, lest all were captured. 'Then my place', said the padre, 'is back there with them.'

'No, no,' answered the men in the boat, 'our signal commanding us to return included you also.' 'I sometimes receive signals', he answered, 'that are more urgent than yours. And I come under a Higher Command.' Before they knew what was happening, the padre had jumped overboard and was swimming back, to certain captivity with the men he hoped to help. The rest watched in silence, until someone said, very quietly, 'I guess it isn't easy to be a Christian.'

The good Christian soldier is always listening for those 'signals more urgent' that come from the Higher Command of Christ.

25 A Taste of Honey

Many centuries ago, when the land of Israel was very short of food, because rain had not fallen, and harvest after harvest had failed to grow and ripen, one old man determined to save his family and his flocks from complete starvation. It hurt his pride to have to appeal to strangers for help, but he felt it must be done. Calling his sons about him, he urged them to go to Egypt, where it was rumoured that large stocks of corn and oil had been laid up in case of famine, and there try to bargain with the Egyptians for food.

He gave them gold, to bargain with; he instructed them carefully on how to approach the leading men in Egypt, what to say, what arguments to use, how to appeal for kindness and mercy towards the hungry, and how not to pay more than they must. Then, as a final persuasion, a simple sign of friendship and goodwill, the old man added 'Take with you a little honey.'

That was really a clever thought, as well as a kind one. Israel was quite famous for its honey. Did you know that the taste of honey is affected by the particular flowers from which the bees gather it? And even by the kind of soil in which the flowers grow! Heather-honey is very slightly sharp, from acid in the peat-soil beneath the heather. Apple-honey has a very special flavour from the orchards where the bees in spring-time help to 'set' the fruit that will swell and ripen in the autumn. Clover-honey, again, is very sweet, with a delicious fragrance all its own. Israel's honey – well, it would have sun-shine in it, and the sweetness of the heavy dews, and some-thing of the beauty of the lovely wild flowers of the Holy Land. Certainly Israel's honey was well known, and in wide demand.

As things turned out, that act of kindness was particularly important. The old man Jacob did not know, nor did his sons, but the man they were to bargain with in Egypt not only came from Israel – he was their own brother! He would recognise the taste, the very special taste, of honey from home. That would make a great difference.

For the Lord High Commissioner for Food in Egypt, Joseph, was the long-lost son of the old man. He had many good reasons for refusing to help these hungry brothers of his: years before, they had sold him into slavery. He had been carried away by traders into Egypt, and there for a while he had been in prison and in even greater danger. But God was with him, and he had won through to a place of great trust and power, second only to the King of Egypt. Now his treacherous brothers were in his power; he could take revenge.

But Lord High Commissioner Joseph was not like that. He thought only of how good God had been to him, in saving his life and bringing him to such a position in Egypt that he could wisely save the lives of others by carefully preserving the stocks of food in a bad time. So Joseph received his brethren, though they did not recognise him; and he was kind to them and helped them. Perhaps the gold helped to persuade him, and their arguments, and their shrunken, starved condition; or perhaps it was mainly that Joseph was such a thoroughly good man. But I am sure the honey from home helped too: the little added extra kindness always tells.

Not very long ago, in a little village church, a minister told this story to the children, one Sunday morning. During the following week a knock came at the minister's door, and when he opened it, there stood a lady, laughing and crying, and both at the same time. She was very short, only about four-feet-and-a-bit high; and the minister knew that she was short in other ways too – short of money, and short of comforts, and a little short of friends. Without a word, she opened her shopping bag and pointed, and there on the top of her little bit of sugar and margarine and a tiny packet of tea and other dull things, lay a pot of honey!

This little lady had been to get her pension, which in those days was not very much. She had then gone on to the little corner-shop kept by one of the members of the church. All that she could afford to buy had been put together by the lady behind the counter and placed in the shabby little bag. On the way home, the little lady had suddenly feared for her purse, and checked to see that it was safe: and so, standing on the pavement, she discovered the lovely surprise – the pot of honey. She felt, as she passed the minister's house, that she simply had to tap the door and tell him what had happened, and recall the text, 'Take with you a little honey', and share her joy.

If the shop-lady could have seen the pleasure which that small kindness had brought to a lonely heart, whose life and whose meals, were usually rather dull, she would have known, too, that the little added extra kindnesses always tells.

26 Famous Ladies with Strange-Sounding Names

Young Tom was an orphan, and a chimney sweep. In fact, he was more of a chimney brush than a chimney sweep, for his work was to climb up *inside* the chimneys in large old houses, where coal fires were still used, and brush down the soot from within. There can be little doubt that Tom shifted as much soot with his hair and his clothes as ever he did with his stick and brush.

Of course it was an unpleasant job, and to make things worse, Tom's master was not kind to him. Sometimes Tom was afraid of the wide, dark chimneys, and he hated the falling soot that got into his eyes and his nose and even into his mouth. Besides, he sometimes got lost. Several chimney-passages would join together inside the thick house walls, and when he tried to climb down again to where he started, Tom did occasionally come down the wrong way, and land in some other room.

Tom did that one day, according to a tale that not long ago *all* boys and girls were supposed to love, and he landed in a lovely white bedroom, white curtains and carpets and walls and bedspread and sheets: and in the middle of all that cleanness, dropped black Tom, covered with soot, kicking and gasping and spluttering soot everywhere. What a mess!

And what a fright!

For, as he scrambled to his feet, a little girl sat bolt upright in bed and *screamed*.

Tom knew he was for it, and he ran and ran, and after him the butler and the gardener and the housemaids and the cook and his master, and everyone else within the sound of that little girl's screams. But who can catch a really frightened boy when he gets a good start?

So Tom got away, and kept on running till he could run no more. He felt awful, not only out of breath, and afraid, and sooty, but very lost and lonely and ashamed. For seeing that little girl's frightened face had made him realise what a terrifying sight he looked. He would have liked to stop and speak and perhaps make friends with her: but how could he? No one would make real friends with a filthy, rough, noisy, uncivilised creature like *him*!.

So – the story goes on and on – Tom dived into a stream and lost his dirty skin so full of soot, and lived a new life with 'the water-babies' (whatever they were), and made friends with the fish, and – but to understand how it all turned out you must read Charles Kingsley's *Water Babies* for yourself.

Among all the strange happenings and people in the story, two of the best known were two odd ladies who took in hand Tom's education. One was called 'Mrs Be-done-by-as-you-did' – could there ever be an odder name than that? She was very stern; she believed that everybody (especially every *boy*) should get what he deserved. So when Tom teased the fish by offering them food, and popped pebbles into their mouths instead, Mrs Be-done-by-as-you-did promised Tom a sweet if he would shut his eyes and open his mouth – and she popped a pebble into *his* mouth too. Ugh! I do hope Tom did not bite on it too hard. But at least he knew now what the fishes felt about so mean a trick.

The other lady, 'Mrs Do-as-you-would-be-done-by', was much kinder in her manner, though she too believed that boys, and girls too, must learn how other people feel about things, and never do to others things they do not like done to themselves.

That is one of the oldest rules of good behaviour in the world. Long, long ago in ancient Egypt, Moses prepared to lead a new and rather quarrelsome nation into a promised land; and one of the laws he gave them to govern their attitude to each other was, to limit revenge and spitefulness to what was strictly *fair* and *just*, ruling out violent temper and unrestrained anger. 'Only an eye for an eye,' Moses said, 'only a tooth for a tooth': do to others no more harm than they do to you: be fair.

It was not a bad rule, so far as it went. Mrs Be-done-by-as-you-did sounds like Mrs Moses, and we may call her stern teaching *an iron rule*.

About four hundred years after Moses, away in ancient China, a great teacher called Confucius invented a rather better rule to govern the way people acted towards each other. 'Do not do to others what you do not want others to do to you.' A little later, the Jews had a rule in almost the same words. And the Greeks also said, 'If anything would make you angry if it were done to you, do not do it to anyone else.' All these are ways of saying, put yourself in someone else's place: do nothing which you would not like them to do to you. We sometimes call this *the silver rule*: it is good, and valuable, but not quite the best rule of all. For it could leave you doing nothing, nothing at all, just *avoiding* doing harm.

So, about eight hundred years after Confucius came Jesus, and he too taught us to put ourselves in the place of others. Only he did not leave it in that negative, 'do nothing you would not like' form. Jesus said, think what you would like the other man to do for you – and do that. Make a list of all the kindnesses you would like to receive, and go out and do them to other people. Do not do *nothing*, for fear you might do harm, for that would leave many needful things undone; be busy, do all you can, all the time, for all the people you can – that way you cannot do harm: for your rule will be, 'All things whatsoever you would that men should do to you, even so do you also unto them. For this is all God's law, and the teaching of his prophets.'

That is Jesus' *golden rule*. Mrs Do-as-you-would-be-done-by had the right idea, after all.

27 Two's a Crowd

I saw two children quarrelling the other day, and they puzzled me greatly, because they were so many.

There was a boy and a girl: they were quarrelling in that special sort of way that goes on and on, each saying hard, unkind, bossy things, yet neither of them walking away and leaving the other alone. That told me they were brother and sister.

I have no idea of their names, so let's call them Jack and Jill. Nor did I hear what they were quarrelling about: I could only watch, and I saw something very odd indeed.

There was one Jack, as Jack saw himself: the boy who, being a boy, of course knew better than any girl, about everything; and who, being a boy, meant everything he said, and *never* changed his mind. But there was another Jack, the one his sister saw: a silly, stubborn boy who would never listen, and whom she could not bend in any way.

And there were two Jills, too. There was Jill as she saw herself, a kind and thoughtful sister, older and therefore wiser than her brother, trying very patiently to teach this silly brother a bit of sense. And there was the Jill whom Jack saw, a bossy, cross, and rather bullying sister, too pig-headed to listen and always wanting her own way.

Two Jacks, two Jills, that makes four of them quarrelling.

But there was also the Jack whom his mummy saw, a darling boy, hardly more than a baby even yet, so full of mischief but so sorry, too, when he had been really naughty. He would be much better behaved if his sister would only leave him alone – the dear boy!

Jack's father saw him a little differently: as rather a pest sometimes, teasing his sister, growing downright disobedient and even stubborn sometimes. Nothing really wrong with him, as yet, but he will need taking in hand before long.

In just the same way, her mother saw Jill as getting rather

tiresome, with her grown-up ways and her air of always knowing best, and tending to put-on her brother, to be hard with him. A dear girl, of course, but she needs watching – if only her father did not spoil her!

And Jill's father? Well, like most fathers, he was probably fond of his daughter, and could see little wrong with her. She was growing up wonderfully fast, and nicely, and becoming a real help in bringing up her brother . . .

So here are four more: father's Jill and mother's Jill, father's Jack and mother's Jack. Eight altogether. Add Jack at his very best, in a good mood, thoughtful and obedient; and Jack at his very worst, bad-tempered and angry; add in also Jill at her best and Jill at her worst, and you have four more – *twelve* altogether.

And do not, I beg you, dismiss my story of the quarrelling twelve as all nonsense: they really were all there, mixed up together in Jack and in Jill. We all of us do truly see ourselves in a light very different from that in which others see us. Each person I know, father, mother, brother, sister, friend, teacher, sees me in his or her own light – and sees a different 'ME'. All are partly true, too; all see part of me, one at a time; and all the 'ME's' they see make up the real ME.

But we have not yet counted in the Jack God sees, and the Jill God sees – the real, complete, mixed up good-and-bad Jack, seen as he is, understood perfectly, and loved completely, by God. And the Jill God sees, understands, and loves, as well. That makes yet another two: *fourteen* altogether.

Make no mistake, when Jesus turned and looked at Peter, he saw Peter as no one else had ever seen him, trying, struggling, fearful, failing, wanting to be better, going to be great: and Jesus loved him. And when Jesus looked at the rich young ruler, he saw him as the young man had never seen himself, and as no one else had ever seen him, either. For Jesus looked steadily, and understood, and loved him, and was sad to see him turn away from the kingdom. We all look very different, from above.

I would like to have intervened between Jack and Jill, and tried to settle their quarrel. But I was afraid, and walked on: there were so many of them!

28 Jesus Abroad

So far as we know, Jesus left his own land only twice: once when he was carried as a baby into Egypt; and once again when he visited the district around Tyre, in Phoenicia, a sea-side country bordering upon Galilee.

That second time was something of a sea-side holiday for Jesus. He had come away from the great crowds and the dangers of Galilee, seeking for a time the secrecy and retirement he needed to think and to pray, and to talk with his disciples. It was an ideal place, with cool and pleasant breezes from the blue Mediterranean sea, and much sunshine, and strange sights and sounds among new people – a 'holiday abroad' in fact. And 'he would have no man know' that he was there.

But it was not to be uninterrupted. Jesus could not be hid. One of the women of the district heard of his coming, and she had a daughter, a young girl whom she dearly loved, who was seriously ill. So she came to the house where Jesus was staying, and pleaded that he would have mercy on her child.

Now that was awkward! In the first place, if Jesus performed a miracle for that mother, that would be the end of secrecy; he would have to leave, and find rest and quiet elsewhere. In the second place, the woman herself was really a 'heathen', that is, the follower of some foreign religion, not the true religion of the Jews. Jesus was sent, he said, as the Messiah of the Jews. He had sent his disciples out a little earlier to preach the kingdom of God to the Jews only. Now someone from the wide world beyond Jewry needed his help: what was he to do?

In the third place, there was no doubt at all that if Jesus did extend his ministry to the pagan peoples, his work among his own people would be ended. No Jew would ever accept as Messiah one who claimed to be sent also to the 'Gentiles'. Many of them thought *they* were the only people God was interested in! – and though Jesus did not think that, he had to

consider the effect of what he did on those he hoped to win for his kingdom. So Jesus said, first of all, 'Let the children' (meaning the Jews) 'first be fed: it is not fitting to take the children's bread and cast it to the dogs.' (Jews sometimes called the Gentiles 'dogs', meaning the wild dogs of the fields and the streets.)

But no mother with a sick child is going to give up that easily. Quickly and cleverly the woman replied, 'Yes, Lord, yet the dogs under the table eat of the children's crumbs!' She meant that it was only a *little* help (a crumb), that she asked, and that for a special pet, her daughter – for she spoke not of the wild dogs of the fields but of the pet dogs that ate beneath the table in the home.

At once Jesus relented. 'O woman, great is your faith! Be it done for you as you desire.' And her daughter was healed instantly: returning home the joyful mother found her daughter well. Jesus had to leave that district right away, and go on secretly to other quiet places. But he did not mind. However puzzled we may be by what he said, we understand at any rate what he did – in spite of his own plans, that brought him such a long and tiring journey seeking rest, in spite of the way his granting her request interfered with his own comfort, Jesus was moved by the mother's love for her child, and even more by her simple, implicit faith in him, and granted her request. His was a love that knew no boundaries: the Jews, and even the disciples, had to learn that sooner or later, whether they liked the idea or not.

Some people even think that the foreign woman's faith, and her earnest, clever argument, may have suggested something new to Jesus himself. He was ever listening for what his Father, God, would say to him, no matter through whom God might choose to speak. It is not impossible that the woman's words, and faith, reminded Jesus of the many thousands outside the Jewish nation who also needed the message of God's love. At any rate, by the end of his ministry, Jesus was speaking of the kingdom of God for all mankind. In his last great commission to the disciples for their work when he had returned to God, Jesus said very plainly, 'Go therefore and make disciples of all nations . . . And lo, I am with you, alway, even to the end of the world.'

Now-a-days we need not go abroad to meet people of other languages than ours, other colours than ours, other nations and other faiths. They walk our streets, attend our schools, and live beside us. It is well to remember the readiness of Jesus to help and to befriend the stranger and the foreigner – despite the questions, and the awkwardness, and however 'different' they may be. Did he not say that if he died for us, he would gather all men unto him?

> Red and yellow, black and white,
> All are precious in his sight –
>   Jesus died for all the children of the world!

29 A Soldier's Faith

The Roman army was one of the finest that the world has ever seen, efficient, well-trained, and well-disciplined. It was divided into 'legions', each of six thousand men; each legion had sixty officers of a special rank called 'centurions', because (as you can see) they commanded one hundred men each (a 'century' of men). The real quality of the army depended on these centurions more than on anyone else.

Though long service in many parts of the world gave some of them a rough appearance and (as an old writer says) 'an un-gentlemanly shape', these centurions were generally fine men, very carefully chosen. We know the kind of men who were preferred – 'not too venturesome, or fond of danger, but with the gift to command others, steady men, and serious, not prone to rush into battle and strike first, but always ready to die in defence of their posts if their men are outnumbered and hard pressed.'

Most of the centurions were extremely brave, contemp-tuous of cowardice and of pain. They were usually very just when they had to punish: their badge was a baton of thin vine-stem, which they could use skilfully as a cane on anybody who misbehaved, or disobeyed an order. Many of them, too, like most Romans, were very superstitious, anxious to know what the stars, or the flight of birds, or the dice, foretold about the future.

Jesus came face to face with at least two such men, with in-teresting results. One paid to Jesus the highest compliment such a man could ever pay to anyone. He was the centurion in charge of the soldiers who put Jesus to death. It was his duty to wait until the end, to keep order, and to make sure that the governor's orders were carried out. So he stayed to watch Jesus die, and he was so deeply impressed with Christ's cour-age and calmness at the end that he commented: 'Truly, this was a just man – a son of God.' Brave men recognise bravery when they see it, and admire it above all else.

The other centurion whom we know Jesus met seems to have been stationed in Palestine, far from his home, for a long time, and he may well have been moved around the world, wherever he was ordered, before that. But rarely can he have served in any place more hostile, or more dangerous. Most of the Jews hated Romans, without limit, hindering them all they dared, insisting to the last detail on all their rights, treating all Romans (when it was safe to do so) with contempt, and longing for the day when Rome and all her forces would be driven from the land. To be a centurion helping to govern such a people, was no easy or pleasant task.

In spite of all that, this centurion had come to have some special feeling for Palestine, and even to admire the faith and the ways of the best Jews. That did happen sometimes: especially because educated and thoughtful Romans found it hard to believe in the many gods of paganism, and turned to the pure faith of Judaism in one God, holy and true. They also envied the Jews their pure and strong home-life, with families loyal to each other and closely knit together. This centurion seems to have felt all that.

So when he came to beg a favour from Jesus, there were leaders from among the Jews to speak up for him. 'He is worthy', they said, 'that you should do this, for he loves our nation, and he has built us a synagogue.' Nor is that all. He was a kindly and good-hearted man towards his servants. The favour he asked was that Jesus should heal a servant who lay paralysed, and in danger of death. Most surprising of all, perhaps, for a Roman officer, he was a humble man. For when Jesus replied that he would come and heal the man, the soldier returned a very remarkable answer.

'Lord, do not trouble yourself, for I am not worthy to have you come under my roof; therefore I did not presume to come to you.' (It seems he had first sent the Jewish leaders to plead for him.) Then the centurion added, with immense confidence in Jesus' authority and power, 'But only say the word, and let my servant be healed. For I am a man set under authority, with soldiers also under me: and I say to one "Go" and he goes; and I say to another "Come" and he comes; and to my slave "Do this" and he does it.' Even so (he implied) if Jesus, too, will only give the order, it will be done!

Luke, writing the story, adds his own comment: 'When Jesus heard this, he marvelled at him, and turned and said to the multitude that followed him, "I tell you, not even in Israel have I found such faith." And when they returned to the house, they found the servant well.'

So Jesus recognised the fine character of a man of another race, whom many people would have hated simply because he was a foreigner, an alien, and a representative of Roman power. So, too, Jesus responded to the appeal of one in need, from whatever land he came. But even more significant, perhaps, is what Jesus said. This time it is not a centurion's compliment to Jesus, but Jesus' compliment to the centurion, that is so striking. 'Not even in Israel' – where one might expect strong faith, in view of all that God through the centuries had done for them – 'Not even in Israel have I found such faith!'

We might expect a soldier's faith to be courageous, daring, unafraid, as we might expect a soldier, above all men, to feel and understand the authority with which Jesus spoke. This soldier's faith was 'great' because of the great difficulties he overcame, the great trust he expressed, the great hostility he had won over to friendship, the great confidence he had in the power of Jesus' word.

When people look, and sound, very different from ourselves, we sometimes forget that they, too, can come to faith in God, that they, too, can receive all that Jesus came to give. For his saving love embraces *everybody*. Most of all, we like to forget, sometimes, that people of other races can not only learn what we learn, but can go on to teach us what we never properly understood, and show us ways of serving Christ that we have never thought of. Jesus said, 'Not in Israel have I found so great faith . . .' as he had met in this Roman centurion. Would he, do you think, ever say, 'I have never found, in any white man, such faith as in this Japanese, this Indian, this African . . .'?

I think he would.

30 An Ancient Quarrel

'The Jews had no dealings with the Samaritans.' We all know that curt summary of a dreadful quarrel, a bitter feud, that divided two peoples living close together in the same land much as Jews and Arabs do today. There were many reasons for that quarrel, which is another way of saying it had gone on so long that people had forgotten the real reason, and imagined, or invented, others – as is the way with people who quarrel. So this story must start far back.

The Samaritans were a 'mixed' people, brought in from other lands and tribes to mix with the native people when foreign rulers occupied Israel; in contrast, Jews were very proud of being descended 'straight' from Abraham. So racial pride came into the squabble, and some contempt for 'impure' ancestry.

The land of Samaria had once been part of the one country of Israel, before a bitter war had divided north from south. Further changes and invasions followed, so that in Jesus' day the whole land had become a sort of sandwich, with the Jewish land of Galilee at the top, Samaria in the middle, and then the Jewish land of Judah at the bottom. Of course, that did not help any: most Jews would prefer to avoid Samaria by going the long way round from south to north or north to south, travelling on the other side of the river Jordan. And each in his heart, Samaritan and Jew, would say about Samaria 'This is our land, and always was!' Thus nationalism came into the squabble.

But especially did religion come into it, as in the quarrel in Ireland today. It was not that the Samaritans were 'heathen', and the Jews were the only worshippers of the true God: it was never so simple as that. For the *Samaritans* possessed the old places where the earliest Jews – Abraham, Isaac, and Jacob – had lived, raised altars, dug wells, and worshipped God; and *they* said that these old places were the right places for worship still. The Jews said, 'No: only at Jerusalem should men offer sacrifice to God.'

What is more, the Samaritans possessed some of the Jewish scriptures, the books of Moses, but the Jews (or most of them) had other sacred books too, the histories of Samuel and David, the Psalms and the prophets, which they reverenced as God's word. Of course, each side said the other was wrong.

Sad to say, religious quarrels are among the bitterest of all quarrels; and very strangely, they can be most bitter when the people we quarrel with are not wholly different from ourselves but only a little different. Sometimes Christians and Hindus can be very polite to one another, yet some Hindus very rude to other Hindus, and some Christians very bitter against other Christians! People who have much in common seem to quarrel most! And so, the Jews had no dealing with the Samaritans.

Except for one Jew – Jesus. Jesus took no notice at all of the ancient feud, and ignored the petty squabbling. When it suited him, he travelled through Samaria, not the long way round. Once when some Samaritan villagers refused to give him hospitality for the night, the disciples were so angry at the 'insult' offered to their Master that they suggested calling down fire from heaven to punish the Samaritans. Jesus simply said, 'Let's go elsewhere.'

When a Jewish lawyer asked Jesus what was the greatest law of all, and was told 'Love God, and love your neighbour', he answered 'But who is my neighbour?' Jesus replied with the memorable parable of the man attacked by robbers and left injured by the roadside. He told how first a Jewish priest, and then a Jewish servant of the temple, simply passed the man by, doing nothing for him; and then how a kindly *Samaritan* came along, and at once took care of the man, bound up his wounds, took him to shelter, and paid for his lodging until he should be well. Your neighbour, Jesus was saying, is anyone near enough for you to help ('neighbour' *means* 'one near'); but he added, by the way he told the story, that the likeliest one to do it was – a Samaritan! That must have made the Jewish lawyer jump!

Another time when Jesus travelled through Samaria he was left alone, the disciples going on to buy food. Being very weary, Jesus sat to rest on the top of that very well which Jacob had dug in Samaria centuries before. There came a Samaritan woman, also alone, to draw water. Usually, a Jewish man and a Samaritan woman would just ignore one another – look the other way. But Jesus, always friendly, actually opened the conversation, and in the very kindest way, by asking for a favour – for a drink from the water she was drawing. That made the woman feel that she was somebody, and somebody important, somebody who could be trusted to be kind.

She was so surprised, and said so. But that led on to a long talk, in which Jesus said that God is Spirit, and is to be worshipped *anywhere* in spirit and in truth: whether it was at Jerusalem or in Samaria did not matter. Jesus also offered the Samaritan woman a gift greater than anything he asked for, the gift of eternal life, springing up within her heart. And he read her troubled, burdened mind, her lonely heart, and told her he was Messiah, come to save.

Excitedly, she left her waterpot and ran back to her neighbours, crying out 'Come, see a man which told me all that ever I did'. A great crowd of the Samaritans then streamed out to the well to see Jesus, and as he talked with them many believed on him, and called him 'Saviour of the world'.

'Of the world': yes, of Jews and Samaritans, of Greeks and Romans, of Negroes and Chinese, and all the rest. All quarrels about race and nationalism, all pride and contempt towards people of another colour or language or culture or land, all disappear if we truly love Christ, our Saviour, and the Saviour of the *world*.

31 It Rains in China, Too

In many parts of the church, baptism is still conducted in the New Testament way, by 'immersing' (that is, dipping beneath a pool of water) those who have confessed their faith in Christ, and are determined to follow him. It can be a most impressive service: but sometimes it can lead to difficulties where there is not enough water, and to complications where there is too much!

It often rains in China, and one particular summer the rain poured down in torrents until the great river Yangtse overflowed through all the houses along its banks and through the city streets in a vast flood. Everyone moved upstairs, or to higher ground if they could, on to the railway embankment, or into whatever boats they could find. Then, near the city of Hankow, a huge dam holding back the river from the city suddenly gave way, and all except the highest ground and the very largest buildings was covered several feet deep.

Within Hankow, a Christian Mission hospital had to make hurried arrangements for the safety of the patients. Beds and tables, instruments and medicines, and finally the patients themselves, all had to be carried upstairs to the dry floors above. Before it was all done, water was coming up between the floorboards down below. A few patients who were well enough wanted to go home to see that their families were safe, and if they could find the high prices charged for boats, they were allowed to go. The seriously ill, the poorer ones, the staff and doctors, nurses and other helpers, all stayed, in a sort of hospital at sea – the upper floors standing up above the flood, and everyone coming and going by boat, and getting in and out through windows!

One patient was a soldier, a fairly high-ranking Chinese officer. While in hospital, he had heard the story of the Lord Jesus, and had spent many hours reading and re-reading a copy of the Gospels. The daily Christian prayer-time had helped him very much, and also some long talks with the hospital evangelist, who had explained that the same Jesus of whom he was reading was still the living Saviour of all men, and his Saviour too, if only he would put his trust in the Lord Jesus. Very gladly the soldier had responded, learning more and more each day of what it meant to be a Christian.

Then came the flood: and the young army Captain felt he must leave at once to rejoin his regiment and lead his men in whatever extra work they had to face. This meant returning to live among thousands of soldiers who would know nothing of the Christian faith or Christian ways, and facing many fierce temptations. So the Captain decided, first, and quite definitely, that he would follow Jesus, all the way; and secondly, and equally definitely, that he wanted to be baptised, and return to his men as an accepted and recognised member of Christ's church.

Of course, the first decision made all the hospital staff deeply happy. So did the second decision – but there were difficulties. One was a rule, and a wise rule, that no new convert should be baptised until he had been a Christian for a year. This was to make sure he understood the gospel, and knew what he was doing, and meant it with all his heart; and to let him gain experience of how much it might cost him to follow Jesus, in persecution or rejection by his family and former friends. But this young Christian Captain wanted to be baptised at once, before he left the hospital.

Hurriedly, a Chinese minister was found, and he came in a borrowed boat, was helped over the window-sill into the hospital ward, and settled down to talk long and earnestly with the young soldier. After many questions, and much explanation, and a time of prayer, the minister agreed to baptise the soldier, although it seemed too soon. He was satisfied that the Captain understood, and really had given his life to Christ.

Then came the next difficulty – too much water! For the hospital chapel was *full* of water, with the baptising pool somewhere down at the bottom, under the flood. Still, everyone was willing and happy, so amidst great fun and joy the top ward was moved about again, beds crowded along the walls, seats brought in and squeezed tightly together, the whole place decorated, Chinese-fashion, with streamers and lanterns and gospel-pictures, and some kind of bath or pool set up for baptism. Presently the minister came again, in through another window, and the service went forward, with hearty praise and real joy. Someone who was there wrote afterwards that the young Captain 'with his bright happy face, told of how Christ Jesus had changed his life, and brought salvation, grace, and purpose into it'. Everything went splendidly, although outside the water still swished by.

Then the Captain left. But before going, he set aside from his savings just enough to see him back to camp, and with the rest he bought from the hospital's bookstall all the Bibles and Gospels he could afford, to take back with him to his men, to tell them of his new-found Saviour. Then he too climbed through the window into a boat, and sailed off: and the hospital slowly returned to something like its normal life.

It was a few years before the hospital staff heard of the Captain again, years in which the Japanese came to China, and war planes droned over many towns and cities. Then news came from a missionary stationed away up country. And wonderful news it was.

He said that a Christian Army Officer had visited him, from a training camp thirty miles away, and told him the story of his treatment in hospital, of his finding the Saviour there, and of the baptismal service in the ward above the water. Now, he said, some of his own men at camp had also accepted the Lord Jesus, and wanted to be baptised: would the missionary help? 'How many are there?' the missionary had asked. 'Sixty' was the reply!

Sixty! That was going to take some arranging. But the missionary called in the local minister again, and together they went off to the camp and there spent some time getting to know these new Christians, teaching them, preparing them for what they were undertaking, and telling them over and over again of the love and power of Christ to help them. In the end, all were accepted for baptism, and plans were made for them to come, all on the same day, over the thirty miles to the little church to be baptised.

More difficulties: the church was small; the local Christians were not going to miss *that* service, but they would have to squeeze in where they could around the sixty converts; and the war planes raided nearly every day, dropping their bombs almost anywhere. For all that, plans went forward. The service was arranged for three o'clock, and the local Christians waited eagerly for the men to come. About noon, while the men were on the way, the air-raid warning sounded and soon the planes were overhead. Would the men be safe? The Christians crowded into the church to pray that God would bring them all safely through. But three o'clock came and went, and four o'clock, and soon it would be evening – and then they saw the thin dark line of marching men coming round a hill. All were safe.

It was dark when the service began in the packed little church. The Captain wanted each man to tell of his faith in Christ – all sixty of them! And he also told his own story. Then the baptising began: no one troubled about the time: two, three hours went by, with singing, prayer, gladness, baptising new Christians into the church of Christ. Then a meal all together, and more talk. Then they had to go back, but once again they bought up all the Bibles, Gospels, and hymnbooks they could find to take back to the camp. Others were going to hear of this wonderful Saviour of the world.

It was a good thing that not very far away, down on the coast, there was a depot of the British and Foreign Bible Society, to provide the Bibles and Testaments so often in demand. It was they who first brought home the story of the baptism above the flood, and the sixty who came through air-raids to witness to their Lord.

32 The Cobbler Goes to College

> Cobbler, cobbler, mend my shoe,
> Get it done by half-past two!

That always seems to me a little rude to the cobbler, and a little unkind, too, to set him a task in a very limited time. But the most famous cobbler – or shoe-mender – in the world did far more than that.

His tiny workroom and his hammers may still be seen, and the deep slate trough in which he steeped his leather. The sign that once swung above the cottage door, worn and charred now, is still preserved in a College library in a great University city. But another university, in another land, bears his name on the lips of those who train there. The sound of his insistent, tapping hammer has gone round the world.

William Carey – for that was his name – was born in Northamptonshire over 200 years ago, and grew up without much money, or much opportunity to go to school, or much desire to go to church. He began to work for the village shoemaker, and walked many miles through country lanes to sell his master's shoes and collect others for repair. One of his work-mates, John Warr, an earnest and persuasive boy, told William over the cobbler's bench the story of Jesus, and so led him into the Christian life.

At once William began to want to learn, and what a student he was! Propping books of all kinds beside the shoes he mended, he read and read and read. On his long journeys delivering shoes, he taught himself languages, Greek, Hebrew, Latin, and later Italian and Dutch. He became a teacher, and a preacher, as well as a shoemaker, and out of the many kinds of knowledge he had gained, he wrote a book of his own, about the different peoples of the world. From the scraps of leather beneath his hand he made a map, not of the countryside around him but of the whole earth.

All the time he dreamed about sending the good news of Jesus to the ends of the world. He did not think simply of going himself – others had already done that. William wanted to persuade all Christian people that they should work together to do this; that many should leave their comfortable homes, and train properly, and travel to the lands where Jesus was not known, and so sharing Christian love, and education, and healing and hope, with all peoples.

In one famous sermon, William pleaded that we should –

Expect great things from God,
Attempt great things for God

and long afterwards it was said that those two ideas made up the best pair of shoes that Carey ever cobbled!

Eventually, William sailed for India, never to return. For the rest of his life he was a missionary, *and* planter, *and* Professor in a College, *and* translator of the Bible (he helped in over thirty different translations) *and* friend of the oppressed and the needy, *and* founder of the great University of Serampore. One of the great Bible scholars of our time wrote a fine tribute to Carey's ability:

'Of all amazing things about Carey, the most amazing was his gift for languages. He tells us of a day in his life. He rose before six in the morning; read a chapter in Hebrew; conducted prayers in Bengali; read a portion of the scripture in Hindustani; after breakfast he did some translating from Sanskrit, and read a little Persian with a teacher; after dinner he translated part of Matthew into Sanskrit; at 6 pm he sat down with a teacher to learn Telinga, and in the evening went on with translating Ezekiel into Bengali. It was said of him that he wore out three teachers in a day. He translated the whole Bible into Bengali, Oriya, Hindi, Marathi, and Sanskrit. He set up his famous printing press and cut the first wooden type with his own hands. This is the man who said to his friends that indolence was his prevailing sin . . . Judged by any standards but his own, he toiled like Hercules. He became the Professor of Bengali, Sanskrit, and Marathi at Fort William College . . .'

But most of all, and always, Carey laboured to bring the

119

message of Jesus to all men, and to show God's love to all the world. He wrote, translated, taught, and preached always for the love of Christ. His dream came partly true: the Society he founded for sending the gospel across the world, with the full backing of the churches at home, is still at work, and within a few years of its starting, fourteen other societies, in England and America, had sprung up – and many more since. And his wider dream, that a day would come when from all parts of the world Christian churches would send representatives to one great council or Conference, to plan together the work of God's kingdom, has come true in our lifetime.

Yet to the end William Carey remained a humble man. 'Let me see, Mr Carey,' said a proud officer to him one day, in very important company, 'were you not once a shoemaker?' 'No sir,' said Carey, 'only a cobbler.' 'If God used me,' he once said, 'no one need despair.' 'I can plod;' he said again, 'few people know what can be done until they try, and persevere in what they undertake.' To another great missionary who visited him in old age, William Carey remarked, 'Mr Duff, you have been speaking about "Dr Carey, Dr Carey", when I am gone, say nothing about Dr Carey: speak rather about Dr Carey's Saviour.'

33 A Friend of a Friend is a Friend

'Mr Reginald White?' said the stranger at the door, a question mark pushing up his eyebrows, and his voice.

'Yes,' I said nervously, for this was unusual. Few people spell out my full name: those who know what it is generally cut it short to 'Reg'; everyone else makes do with my initials. So, when he said 'Mr Reginald White' in that formal way, something cowardly inside me whispered 'Police'. Yet I could not think of any wrong I had done just recently.

However the stranger just said 'Good!' quite cheerfully, and asked if he might come in. As we sat down together, he went on, 'You were in – – – until about nine years ago, I believe, and before that you were at – – –'. That was all correct, but still more mystifying. 'Who on earth are you?' I asked – but more politely than that, of course. And he said, 'I am from New Zealand. We have not met. In fact I have never been in this country before.' 'Then how in the world do you know me?' I wanted to ask, but perhaps I did not need to: the look on my face showed my complete bewilderment.

Then the stranger said, 'You know Mr So-and-so . . .' and everything became clear. Of course I knew Mr So-and-so, very well indeed, and soon we were discussing mutual friends, news, the children's progress at school, weddings, books, and went on chatting for an hour.

That is the wonderful thing about friendship: a shared friend makes a new friend. Any friend of a friend is a friend to me, until the chain is endless.

I sat once at a wedding 'breakfast' in a *Chinese* restaurant in London, with a very happy wedding party. A young *Scottish* friend of mine had just been married to a lovely *Japanese* girl, and a great circle of his friends, and her friends, and our friends, had come to share their day.

On one side of me sat a *Welsh* lady, and on the other a young man from Chinese *Formosa*. At the bottom of the table sat the lady and gentleman with whom the bride had been staying: they were from *Germany*, though they had come to London via the *United States* and brought greetings from friends there. Two of the other people present had first met in *Russia*. I think I am right in saying that another guest was from *Holland* (though I may be wrong); and because the bride was a nurse in one of the London hospitals, fellow nurses were represented – I seem to remember, by a nurse from *Jamaica*. Certainly, the two ladies who sat opposite me were *English*: they had taught the bride her first English lessons at home in Japan, where they had been missionaries.

A cosmopolitan breakfast: and we all talked at once, I remember, each of us listening to the language (or languages) he happened to know. But how we talked – with news, greetings, enquiries, comments, from all around the world.

And yet that company had never met before. Nor, so far as I know, have most of them met since. Gathered from so many nations, races, and corners of the world, we ate so many varied foods, and talked in many languages, and laughed together (in the same language!) as friends do. A little earlier, at the wedding service, we had sung together too, and prayed together for the happy pair.

That was the whole secret. From so widely separated places we were drawn together as friends of *him* and *her*, and all of us were also in some measure at least, friends of Christ. And a friend of my friend is a friend to me: especially a friend of my friend Jesus. He can make the whole world *one*.

As we motored home from that lovely 'breakfast', threading our way through London's traffic, a saying of Jesus kept echoing in my mind. He often spoke of the kingdom of God as a wedding feast. Once he added: 'And men will come from east and west, and from north and south, and sit at table in the kingdom of God.'

Nothing in all the world binds together men and women, boys and girls, of all nations and peoples and tongues, like sharing together in the love of God through Jesus our Lord. Truly, and indeed, every friend of my Friend is a friend to me.

34 Into All the World

When Jesus said to his disciples, 'Go ye into all the world . . .'
he did not mean to *explore* the world, but (as indeed he added)
'to preach the gospel to every creature'. Yet it is remarkable
how very much the story of the exploration of the world owes
to the lives of great Christians, and how often the motive for
exploring has been the service of Christ.

Even in New Testament times, Christians seem to have
been ardent globe-trotters, always on the go. Aquila and
Priscilla moved from Rome to Corinth, and on to Ephesus;
Lydia went from Thyatira to Philippi; Paul dodged about all
over the place; Peter travelled the coast as far as Caesarea;
John got to Ephesus, and many believe that Thomas got to
India. Others went to Antioch to found a church, and somehow the gospel was taken to Alexandria in Egypt, to Crete, to
the Black Sea (facing Russia), and to Ethiopia. Considering
that their cars, jets, and Concordes were horses, sailing ships,
and camels, they managed to get about the world pretty well.

About a hundred years after Jesus, a great Christian leader
known as Justin the Martyr explained the astonishing spread
of Christianity in his time by pointing out that everywhere, in
the great cities and on board ship, in the seaports and the
great business houses, men came across Christians, pure of
life, honest of purpose, true of word, kindly of heart, good to
meet and good to know. They were traders, workmen,
travellers, whose changed lives, constancy, and patience won
new converts everywhere. That is a fine tribute.

Already in Justin's time, traders threaded their way
through the Red Sea to India for pepper, spices, perfume,
ivory, pearls and silver, and even beyond to China. This is the
only explanation we have for the existence, very early, of
Christian groups in southern India.

In the fourth century, Frumentius established a church on
the sea coast of Ethiopia; and by the sixth century, a merchant

124

of Alexandria, called Cosmas, decided to combine his business and his faith by visiting Christians on his long voyages to India, Ceylon, Malabar, and beyond Bombay. So Cosmas linked the scattered churches, by news and greetings, always urging distant groups to pray constantly for their neighbouring groups. About the same time, Columba brought the Christian message from Ireland to Iona, off the coast of Scotland, in small boats (coracles) little more than six feet long.

Viking ships from Oslo, in the tenth century, brought a fair-headed giant named Olaf Trygvason, leading pirates to the Scilly Isles off the south coast of Cornwall. There Olaf met a Christian hermit, and after teaching and prayer, he was baptised. Olaf returned to England later, no longer to rob and destroy, but to visit the Christian Bishop at Winchester to gain approval: then he returned again to Norway, where he became the first Christian king, in 995. With his encouragement and help, Christian teachers soon travelled from Oslo to Iceland, Greenland, Shetland and to Orkney.

We know that the great Marco Polo visited the Emperor, Kublai Khan, in Peking at the end of the thirteenth century, bearing letters from Christians in Italy and a message from the Pope. That was an astonishing journey six hundred years ago. One hundred years later, Vasco da Gama was the first to find the way round the southern tip of Africa to reach India, going (as he said) 'to find Christians and spices'. I am glad he put Christians first!

Just before that, Christopher Columbus, as we say, 'discovered America'. In fact, the great continent of the western Atlantic was known to Norwegian sailors nearly five hundred years before; and Columbus did not land on mainland America until after John Cabot, from Genoa, had found it. But the first American-island landing was made by the Columbus party from Spain on Friday October 12th 1492. The leaders of the party carried banners bearing the Cross, and the landing place was called (at first) San Salvador, land of the 'Holy Saviour'. The purpose of the whole vast, dangerous enterprise of crossing the unknown Atlantic in sailing ships was to extend the empire of Christ, or as they put it, 'To let Christ rejoice in the salvation of the souls of so many nations hitherto lost'.

True, there were other motives at work. 'The extension of

our faith and the extension of our wealth' were both mentioned. Spanish pride of empire was in it too; and so was the strange wish to find a way westward to India. Yet Columbus believed, too, that all mankind were loved and saved by Christ, and he wanted them to know it.

Soon afterwards, the Christian Prince Henry of Portugal was pushing southwards down Africa's coast, seeking a way eastwards into that unknown land; and one of his reasons was 'to make increase in the faith of the Lord Jesus Christ'.

In this long saga of restless, exploring Christians, Carey must at least be mentioned, and his pioneering Christian missions in India. But nearer to our own time is the cotton-spinning lad from the tiny home at Blantyre, near Glasgow, who by enormous effort and relentless determination became Dr David Livingstone. A book by a German missionary fired Livingstone's heart with thoughts of China, but a war hindered that intention, and his missionary society sent him instead to Africa.

When he arrived, the great central stretch of Africa was 'either a mere blank, or a bewildering maze of false and nonsensical geography'. When Livingstone died, its main areas had been mapped out, its 'marvels, riches, and horrors' laid bare, and the way opened up for education, healing, and Christian evangelism, across thousands of square miles. The whole Livingstone epic – his seven hundred miles by ox-cart, his escape (quite literally) from an enraged lion's jaws, his crossing of the great Kalahari Desert, his discovery of the mighty Zambesi river, and the great treks across wholly uncharted forest and jungle, his triumph over repeated illness and disaster, together with his active opposition to Africa's horrible slave-trade, his steadfast refusal to break his word to his African servants, and his determination to press on to new areas, measuring and mapping all the way – is one of the great adventure stories of the world.

Through Livingstone's work, a new Christian mission came into being, and in all he did and suffered (as he himself declared): 'Never have I ever appeared as anything but a servant of God, who has simply followed the leadings of his hand ... I feel that I am not my own, that I am serving Christ ... Having by his help got information which I hope will lead to more abundant blessing being bestowed on Africa than ever before.'

Finally, within our own time the Christian exploration of the world has continued in South America, where again Christians were in the forefront, penetrating along the vast Amazon river, and into inland Ecuador, where no white man had ever been. Both attempts cost dearly in the lives of brave men, but as one reporter remarked, they are inspiring reminders that 'the peculiar power and God-given courage which historically have spread Christianity to earth's every remote corner, are still very much alive'.

'The earth is the Lord's, and the fullness thereof' said the psalmist; 'Go ye into all the world' commanded Jesus. Of course, not every Christian can travel far – or at all; and very few can be pioneer explorers. But it is very plain that no one can be Christian and *small-minded*. To follow Jesus, you have to 'think big', because his kingdom, like God's love, encircles the world.

35 In First

We had walked a long way, about twenty miles if I remember rightly, and the day was very hot. We were eight young men, six of us at a time pulling a trek-cart loaded with a tent, blankets, clothes, some food, a small organ, and drawn by a central shaft and long white ropes. For four or five weeks we had been walking through villages and towns, visiting churches sometimes, but much more often holding services in the open air, in town squares, river-sides, fields, parks, hillsides, telling out the story of the Lord Jesus.

It was all good fun, a fine and useful holiday, very healthy and very hot. Heat meant thirst: walking made us thirsty, talking made us thirsty, preaching made us thirsty, singing made us thirsty, perspiring made us thirstiest of all. We needed a drink.

At one bend in the road there was a sudden shout, the shaft of the trek-cart was dropped with a bump, the ropes were thrown aside, and we sprinted together for a tiny village green, just ahead. For there in the centre of the green stood a village pump, and beneath it an ancient stone horse trough, filled with water.

The first man to the pump seized the long, curved iron handle and pumped it up and down, up and down. Nothing happened. Another tried, more slowly. Then another, quietly, coaxingly, but still nothing happened. And there we stood, a ring of bronzed and healthy young men, parched with thirst, around a village pump that simply refused to give us a drink.

We scratched our heads, of course, but that did no good at all. We argued a little, half-heartedly, some saying that the pump was dry because of the heat, others pointing to the dirty water in the trough to show that the pump did work sometimes. Someone suggested singing to it; one of us tried talking to the pump in Welsh; one lad even muttered 'Let's pray': still nothing happened.

An old man on a kitchen chair beside a cottage door called out to us, and pointed to the pump; but as he spoke only in Welsh, and had no teeth, it meant nothing to most of us.

But our one Welsh lad replied to him in Welsh, and we walked over to his chair. The old man repeated his advice, which was translated to us as 'I doubt you'll have to put something in before you'll get anything out!'

That seemed sensible, but put in what? We looked for a slot to put in pennies, but of course there was none. Just as we turned to ask the Welsh lad to seek more intelligible instructions, a lady appeared from behind the cottage. She strode, rather angrily I thought, across the green, looked round the ring of lusty, healthy, helpless young men with withering scorn for our ignorance and uselessness, then bent to take the rusty tin from the trough and empty its contents down the main pipe of the pump. With a toss of her head she turned back, flinging two curt words over her shoulder – 'Now try'.

We did, and after a few rises and falls of the handle, the water gushed all over our feet, soaking our shoes and socks, which made the old man cackle with laughter. As we looked across at him, mugs in hand, he cackled still more, nodding his head vigorously and repeating (I suppose): 'I doubt you'll have to put something in before you'll get anything out.'

The real trouble, as I expect you have guessed, being much more clever than we were, was the hot dry weather. Somewhere down in the main pipe of the pump was a piece of leather that ought to lie flat over a small hole and form an air valve, shut when the pump-rod rose (so drawing up water) and open when the pump-rod fell (so letting through air). The small piece of leather was, like ourselves, hot, dry and thirsty: once wetted by the water poured *in*, it worked splendidly.

One of us remembered, in the tent that night, how someone had written to another young man, who often scratched his head over problems that puzzled him, 'Take your share of suffering, as a good soldier of Christ Jesus. No soldier on service gets entangled in civilian pursuits, since his aim is to satisfy the one who enlisted him. An athlete is not crowned unless he competes according to the rules. It is the hard-working farmer who ought to have the first share of the crops. Think over what I say . . .'

E

Soldier, athlete, farmer – I wonder what Timothy 'thought over' as he pondered Paul's advice. The good soldier must *put in* all his courage and energy and training, if he is to please his officer; the athlete must *put in* strict and prolonged discipline, learning the rules of his sport, before he can hope to win; the farmer must *put in* hours, days, weeks, even months of labour before he can hope to win a harvest. And so, Paul was saying to Timothy – so must the Christian *put in* all he has, if he would please Christ.

For after all, Christ *put in*, first, all he had, to win our salvation, before he was raised by God to sit at his own right hand. 'I doubt you'll have to put something in before you'll get anything out' – of anything worth while.

36 Noah's Ark – in Paris

Most children have very big ideas of what they want to be when they grow up. Sometimes their parents are dismayed by children's hopes – they wonder how they are ever going to prepare, or to provide, for all their children plan to do.

A poor French pig-farmer had just such a dreaming lad. The ground he worked was not very fertile, and the weather in his part of France was not very kind, so the farmer had to work very hard just to pay his way. Yet his son, Vincent, wanted to be a minister, a 'priest' as the French would say. Of course Vincent's father liked the idea of having a son learned, and respected, and a priest of God. But who was to pay for his training, and his fine clothes, and his books?

There was only one thing to do. The work of the farm was helped by two rather thin but useful oxen, who pulled small ploughs and sometimes the tiny cart about the farm. To let them go would mean still harder work for Vincent's father, but what else was to be done? The oxen were sold; the money paid for Vincent to start at the College of Toulouse, and thereafter Vincent had to study and to teach at the same time, earning just enough to finish his course.

Studies completed for the time, Vincent set out for home again, a long and dangerous journey in his days, in the sixteenth century. And sure enough, trouble came. He had decided to come part-way by sea, for that was cheaper, but the ship was attacked by pirates, and Vincent was captured, taken off to North Africa, and sold as a slave, to work for a fisherman. He knew nothing about fishing, so soon he was sold to a farmer: at any rate Vincent knew about farming.

But God had another reason for that change of master. The farmer had once been a Christian, though now he had almost forgotten all about Christ. He had become careless, even sinful: and among other rather odd things he did was to marry three wives, *at once*.

131

In that household Vincent went about his work cheerfully enough, although he was far from home, and a slave instead of a priest. He used to sing in the fields as he worked, and one day the third wife of his master heard him singing, and was puzzled by the song. It was, in fact, one of the Psalms, 'How can I sing the Lord's song in a strange land?' – which seems an appropriate one for Vincent to ponder. When he explained what it meant, and whence it came, the lady asked to be told more, and in due time Vincent told her all about the story of the Bible, the coming of Jesus, and his life and death for us. This won her completely to the way of Christ.

As her husband saw the difference which Christian faith made in her, his own conscience was awakened, and he too came to follow Christ again. As a reward for bringing such blessing to his home, the master set Vincent free. Vincent began again to teach, and to save for the journey home. Soon he was appointed tutor in a great household, where he was well treated, and began to taste a life of wealth and comfort. But before long he began to feel that this was wrong *for him*, because he should be working for God, not himself.

So Vincent changed to harder work, in much less pleasant surroundings. He became a minister to prisoners, first of all, so mixing with some of the roughest, wildest, most violent men. Then he became a minister among slaves – but that leads to another story altogether! In due time Vincent returned much nearer his home, to Paris. Here almost any kind of Christian work was open to him, as a man trained for the priesthood: but he chose to minister again to the poorest, roughest, less responsive and less grateful people, among the very poor streets and bad houses of the city. Among all the people he served, many of them sick, and sad, and wicked, many children without parents, many criminals without hope, most of all he cared about those without homes, or families, or people to love them.

At first with only two friends, later with very many helpers, Vincent set about *organising* long-lasting help for all in need – he did not believe that doling out money-gifts was sufficient to solve anyone's problems. Hospitals, orphanages, training schools, work, and in numerous other ways, Vincent provided what might lead the unfortunate and the helpless to try again, and make something good of their lives. Soon others saw how right he was, and greatly admired his foresight and his energy. He was given a great house in Paris for his headquarters, and there he gathered everybody willing to help, or needing help, that he could find – boys and girls of the streets, a few sick people waiting to go into hospital, teachers, the homeless, rich people anxious to work with him, other priests offering service for a short time, noble men and women, once proud but moved with his own compassion, the high and the lowly, all gathered together. This was the place he called his 'Noah's Ark', because of the mixture of people who stayed there. And because, like the real Noah's Ark, it was a place of rescue.

Apart from the educated, and gentle, people who came to scrub and cook and tend the sick, and teach the children, many other important people offered help, and Vincent was soon organising new and better homes for hundreds of homeless throughout the city. There seemed no end to the work needing to be done, and no end either to the things that Vincent attempted. But all the time, he would not ask others to do what he did not do himself: and night after night he would walk the dingy, dangerous streets and alley-ways gathering homeless boys and girls into his care.

As he grew older, many of the friends who gathered round him wanted to care for Vincent himself, making things easy for him, waiting upon him, shielding him from harm. But Vincent could never forget how God had arranged his life, letting him be captured and sold so that he might learn for himself how the poor, and prisoners, and slaves really felt. He never lost the sense of wonder that he, a very poor farmer's boy, should become the friend of great people, the helper of so many, and used by God. He did not want to be waited upon, he felt so grateful.

'That I – I – the son of a swineherd', he used to say, 'should ever ride like a Prince!'

I think it was worth selling those two oxen, don't you?

37 Vincent – Again!

When someone mentions, in the middle of a story, a promising episode or event that would take a little time to tell, and brushes it away with 'but that's another story', then some sort of promise seems to be implied, to tell it another time. And promises should be kept. So here goes.

We were talking of Vincent (Vincent de Paul, to give him his full name), the French pig-farmer's son whose training for the Christian ministry was paid for by the sale of two much needed oxen. We told how he was captured by pirates and sold into slavery, but eventually became a minister to prisoners, and then to slaves – that is the story. It is quite simple and short, but very significant, and in fact is the story which everyone remembers best of all about 'Saint' Vincent (as most people call him).

Most of us have seen films, or television pictures, of the old sailing ships with lines of half-naked rowers below decks, stretching and pulling at enormously long oars, either to assist the wind or to drive the ship forward when there was no wind at all. Usually they look rough and sullen men, often chained to the oars or to one another; and quite often we see a still stronger, wilder-looking man striding a raised passage between them, shouting oaths at any 'lazy' rowers and wielding a long and wicked-looking whip. It may be all imagination now: once it was very near the truth.

These were the 'galley-slaves', and for many centuries most of the trade, and the naval warfare, of the world depended upon finding enough of them to keep the great ships moving. Many of them were captured in war, to spend the rest of their lives as prisoners striving at the oars. Others, like Vincent, had been kidnapped by pirates and sold to ships' captains as slaves, or to other employers unwilling to pay decent wages. Still others were criminals, or men supposed to be criminals, who were condemned by the courts to serve in

the galleys for so many years, or for life, or (which amounted to the same thing) 'until they could prove their innocence'. It was a dreadful life: the slaves were almost starved; no one cared for them, or dared to defend them; if any became too ill to work he was simply thrown overboard.

The story concerns one such young man, condemned by a court to serve in the slave-ships, but continually protesting that he was innocent – he had done nothing wrong. Often he sobbed the whole day through, thinking of his young wife and their new baby, born just before he was arrested. He was desperately anxious about them, and how they would find food and lodging without him to earn for them; and he longed to be with them. But the more he sobbed, the more the slave-master whipped his shoulders 'for being lazy', determined to 'beat the nonsense out of him'. One by one the young man saw those around him collapse from exhaustion, and watched them carried away to be thrown over the side: then one day the man rowing in front of him simply died in his seat, and was left there a day and a night, for some reason, before he too was removed. The young man saw it all, and fell into the bitterest despair.

But the next day a miracle happened. As he sat, staring into space, someone spoke to him: 'Good morning, my son.' Looking up, he saw – of all things on such a ship – a shabbily dressed priest. This was Vincent, who by long argument, and by pressure on the government officials in the seaport at Marseilles, had got himself appointed as chaplain and minister to the slaves. Someone had told him of the young man, and very probably he had had to bury the man who had died, since that had happened in port. So here he was, to talk to the young man, and to listen to his protest of innocence for himself, and see what he could do. In fact he had already formed a plan, and when he heard the story, he acted at once.

After a short talk, Vincent said to him – 'Well, stand up, and hold out your arm.' Then he motioned to a man beside them, and the chain was unlocked; to the utterly astonished young man Vincent said quietly, 'You are free, my son. Go home to your family in peace, and serve God in humbleness all the days of your life.' It need hardly be said that he asked no questions, but fled.

What happened next astonished the whole ship. For the priest quietly sat down in the young man's place, and held out his arm for the chain! That is what the chaplain had arranged. If he was satisfied that the story was true, he would take his place and set him free. Why did the Captain agree? Vincent was not easy to oppose, once his mind was made up; perhaps the slave-master thought it would be fun to have a priest among the slaves – he could boast of it in the drinking dens of Marseilles; or perhaps he thought that the young man was too soft and always sobbing, and the priest could be made to row better than the stupid boy. Whatever the reason, the thing was done, and Vincent had become, no longer a fisherman's slave, or a farmer's slave, but a galley-slave.

Of course the other slaves thought him mad. Some cursed him; some were afraid of him – he represented God! But he spoke gently to them all. He tore up pieces of cloth to roll around the chains where men's arms or legs were bleeding from the chafing, day after day. Whenever they were near enough to land to hear a church bell call to evening prayer, the priest – still working – would pray aloud: though at first many jeered and cursed, in time the ship would fall silent each time he prayed, and some would pray with him. Many wished that someone would do for them as he had done.

And what a fund of stories Vincent had to help through the long days and the longer nights: stories of his own childhood on the farm, awakening in some of the slaves memories of their own homes; stories of the heroes and martyrs of the church, things he had learned in his training to be a priest, that now came in useful to share with these poor and ignorant men. He even sang sometimes, the songs of worship and the Psalms, and a few of the men who once had been in church choirs as young boys, sang and wept with him.

Sometimes he was whipped, and always took it without flinching, as the other slaves noticed. Once or twice, when others should be whipped, Vincent insisted on taking the whipping himself, promising that the offender would work in future. But here a difficulty arose: for the slave-master was secretly a little afraid to whip this man of God; and he became aware that if he went on doing so, he might have a riot of the whole galley on his hands. Yet if he did not whip Vincent, and let off those whom Vincent defended, how could he keep order? He began to regret agreeing to the exchange.

Besides, the word got around, and when the ship arrived in Marseilles after each voyage, crowds would gather at the quayside to see this galley-slave-priest, to hear prayers being said in the galley, and the slaves singing! It was rather surprising – and, when you thought of it, rather wonderful. What a change one man had made!

Whether the government officials who appointed Vincent chaplain came to hear of the crowds on the quayside, and of their priest acting as a slave; or whether the slave-master was glad to be rid of him; or whether some other church officials intervened – we do not know, but Vincent was dismissed from his new job, and left for Paris.

But Marseilles never forgot the story of Vincent de Paul, and the Christian compassion that made him take the place of the young slave to set him free. It is the story most often told about 'Saint' Vincent. But we said also that it was *significant*. Can you see why? It was not only that for the first time for many people, a clear example of what Christian love will do had been set before their eyes. There was more to it, even than that. For people saw that *this was just what Jesus had done*. He too had come beside us, of his own free choice, to take our place as sinners, and 'sit in for us', accepting all that we deserved, that he might set us free. 'He was wounded for our transgressions, bruised for our iniquities; the chastisement of our peace was upon him, and by his stripes we are healed. He was numbered with the transgressors, and bare the sin of many . . .'

> Bearing shame and scoffing rude,
> In my place, condemned, he stood,
> Sealed my pardon with his blood –
> Hallelujah, what a Saviour.

Watching 'Saint' Vincent, men understood the gospel better, and then they understood what made Vincent do it.

Nothing finer than that could be said of any man.

38 Leonardo Da Wonder Boy

That was not his real name, of course. He was Leonardo Da Vinci, born in a little village in Italy over five hundred years ago. But 'wonder boy' he certainly was, probably the cleverest man who ever lived: not the wisest, the best, or the greatest, but undoubtedly the cleverest. Some called him 'the greatest light of the whole period of Enlightenment', one whose 'many-sided genius is unique in the history of the world'. Another said it another way: 'Leonardo's "versatility" (many-sided gifts) has never been paralleled in the history of the world.'

So we are not exaggerating, if we call him 'wonder boy'.

It seems hardly fair that any man should have so many gifts, so much 'going for him'. His face was striking, even handsome, framed by long golden curls down to his shoulders; his body was athletic, full of energy, exceedingly strong – he could bend horseshoes in his hands; his voice was 'spellbinding' when he spoke in public, and as a poet, lute-player and singer, making up his own songs as he went along, he entertained 'most divinely'.

As a young man, he made himself a lute almost wholly of silver, in the shape of a horse's head, which produced a tone of 'amazing sweetness and force'. In school he may have been something of a nuisance, for he loved arithmetic, and understood it so well that he often raised questions which no one at all could answer.

Yet drawing and modelling were his chief interests at first: it is said that his teacher once threw down his brushes in despair of teaching Leonardo anything. By the time he was twenty, he was acknowledged an independent painter (no longer someone else's student) by the Guild of Painters in the city of Florence. Soon he was carving sculptures, too. One of his new ideas, copied by most later artists, was to try to show not only the shape and colours of things, but how the light and shade fell on them. To do this properly he studied the laws of light, and 'optick glasses', and how our eyes work. He actually compared the way that sound and light waves travel with the way that waves travel in the sea: we thought *that* idea came with modern science!

For his sculpture, with the same thoroughness, Leonardo studied anatomy in animals and in humans, how muscles and nerves and joints and bones all work together, so that his marble figures should 'look as though they could move'. These studies led Leonardo into science of all kinds. He studied the conduct of war, and offered his ruler some new ideas for the planning of battles. Later he designed a new kind of cannon. But he did not like war, and painted one marvellous picture to expose what he called 'the bestial frenzy of battle'.

Moving to another city, Milan, around a time of plague, Leonardo drew plans for building a new city with wider, cleaner streets and better sanitation. For a while he gave much attention to architecture, constructing and improving public buildings; and to the science of hydraulics (the use of water-power), planning water-ways, the irrigation of farm-fields, and many canals. This in turn led him to study the tides, and the rocky surface of the earth; and also the changes in the weather, especially the mystery of thunder and lightning.

He moved on to investigate geography scientifically, and to exquisite map-drawing: some of his maps are still treasured in a royal library. As if earth was not big enough to study and to draw, he added astronomy to his investigations, along with geometry, dynamics, and more arithmetic. In his 'spare' time, he still wrote poems, stories, songs, and conducted pageants, arranged festivals!

Of all these studies, through forty years, Leonardo kept endless detailed notebooks (doesn't he make you tired!). It is said that if these notes had ever been published, scientists 'would have been saved centuries of labour'; for much that was later discovered or invented by others was foreseen by this amazing man. He studied ships, for example, and invented a new way of propelling them by paddle-wheels; he suggested ways by which steam could be used to provide power; he pioneered the study of leaves and flowers, drawing

them minutely and accurately; he drew a ship which might travel under water – a submarine! – and he designed aeroplanes which if he had had some driving power like the modern petrol engine, 'might have flown'.

Yet, in spite of all these scientific marvels, Leonardo is best remembered as the painter of the portrait 'Mona Lisa', perhaps the best-known painting in the world; and of Jesus at the Last Supper, which some think the greatest painting in the world, and of many others.

Surely so gifted, so clever, so 'miraculous' a man must have been very proud, spoiled by success in so many things. Not a bit of it. Those who knew Leonardo well called him charming, popular, and deserving to be; a generous friend to many people; and always loyal to his friends and pupils. Perhaps this was partly because he remembered his rather poor beginning, in a 'broken' home: his mother left him when he was a child, and he was brought up by his father only.

But we must remember also that he understood deeply the heart of Christian teaching: he who understood so many things better than his generation, also understood Jesus. His painting of Mary and the Infant Jesus so moved all who saw it that the room where it was hung was filled with men and women, silent, many of them kneeling, for two whole days without a break. His painting of Jesus at the Last Supper was so astonishingly powerful and beautiful that the French king wished to cut away the thirty feet of convent wall on which it was painted, to carry it away to France.

For that great painting, Leonardo had seized on the very moment when Jesus warned that one of the disciples would betray him. All the disciples are seen as shocked, upset, dismayed; only Jesus is shown to remain sublimely calm, unafraid, and tender. To Leonardo, it seems, that terrible danger of betraying Christ was so awful that it called out all his skill and cleverness, his understanding and his power.

Leonardo was clever enough to know that cleverness is not enough. Even the cleverest needs character, too, and faith, and loyalty to Christ. To worship the infant Jesus; to be faithful to Christ about to die for us – these thoughts called for his utmost concentration and produced the very best among all his stupendous achievements.

39 Nineteen men – and Asahel

After King Saul's death, there happened in Israel the first of many bitter civil wars; wars, that is, not between two different peoples but between two parts of the same people. These are surely the most tragic and terrible wars of all.

In this war, David's supporters were fighting the followers of a rebel leader called Ish-bosheth. David's men were led by his own nephews, Joab, Abishai, and Asahel, three brothers, of whom Asahel was only a youth. Ish-bosheth's men were led by an ambitious old soldier named Abner.

At one point in the battle, Asahel rather rashly challenged Abner to fight the quarrel out just between themselves. He had no chance for Abner was experienced, and very strong. To be fair to Abner, he did not want to kill the boy, but urged him to fight someone his own age. But Asahel persisted, and so he died.

Recording the history of it all, long afterwards, the Bible tells how, when it was all over, 'all who came to the place where Asahel had fallen . . . stood still . . . And when Joab had gathered all the people together, there was missing of David's servants *nineteen men beside Asahel*'.

Who then were the nineteen? We do not know. Why single out Asahel to be named like this, the only name remembered? For altogether and counting both sides, three hundred and eighty men were killed that day. Why then is young Asahel, alone, remembered by name?

There are two answers. One is, that Asahel was someone special. To have been one of the commanders, at so young an age, suggests that he was brilliant, a leader already for other men, even though somewhat rash. The story of his death reveals how very brave he was, and how persistent. Besides, this old idea of settling the quarrel by one personal combat, as David's fight with Goliath settled for a time Israel's quarrel with the Philistines, though it seems a very strange method to us, was really a good idea. It could have saved so many lives: that seems to have been Asahel's intention, and shows again the kind of man he was. Clever, brave, persistent, ready to risk his own life to save others: Asahel was someone special.

When we hear of great tragedies of any kind, an airplane crashing, or an earthquake, people dying of famine, or in some furious hurricane or disastrous flood; or when in November we recall the thousands who were killed in two World Wars, it is *very* hard to remember that every single one was someone special. No two people are exactly the same. Each person has his or her own thoughts, and hopes, his or her own joys and memories and loves; his or her own hobbies, and interests and abilities. No one, *no one at all*, is just one of thousands, or one among hundreds, or one of the ten. Every single one is special: it should have been nineteen names and Asahel.

Sometimes, when we are arguing about the great cost and wastefulness of war, we list the brave and gifted people, Germans, Americans, Russians, British, Japanese, Koreans or whatever they were, who never returned home: doctors, nurses, scientists, musicians, poets, writers, teachers, leaders and the rest, who never lived to do their real work for the world. That is true – that is why war *is* wasteful and horrible and cruel. But it is not just certain gifted, and clever people who are special and precious. God counts *everyone* a special person, an 'Asahel' in his sight, and loves her, loves him, as an only child. That is one of the clear things Jesus taught us, that every single person matters to God.

But secondly, Asahel was someone's brother. He was Joab's younger brother, and Joab was David's leading general, a great man in the land. That was why, before the army dispersed and the men returned home, David's followers stopped to bury Asahel, and marked the place carefully.

But then everyone is someone's brother, or sister, or son or daughter, or father or mother, or husband or wife: everyone is a relative of someone, with very few (and very sad) exceptions. Each life wounded, or lost, amid hundreds, or thousands, spreads sorrow through a circle of people. Paul said that no man lives to himself, and no man dies to himself; though some have very lonely lives, and some even die alone, that is because things have gone very wrong for them. Actually, we all belong to someone; we are 'bound in the bundle of life' with those who gave us birth, and with many others too. We all 'belong' to God.

Someone special, and someone's brother: so Jesus taught us to look on everyone around us. God loves the world, and all are his. As the Bible says, again, 'God has made of one blood all nations of men to dwell on the face of the earth.' All therefore are brethren 'under the skin'. Following Jesus we learn to 'rejoice with those who do rejoice, and weep with those who weep', trying very hard never to lose sight of the *one* amidst the *crowd*. Because God never does.

And, other people apart, it is a great thing to carry always, deep in your own heart, the inner knowledge that *you* are someone special to God, that you *belong* to him, are his child. There are days when to know that makes a very great difference.

40 Bouncebackability

The little man was not very impressive, and certainly not frightening. Besides being short, he was bow-legged, and had a rather high squeaky voice. His bushy eyebrows met above his hooked nose, which would hardly make him handsome. And he peered short-sightedly at you, as though he had difficulty in seeing you at all. A somewhat ordinary-looking man, one you might easily pass by in a crowd without even noticing, let alone remembering.

The little man came one day to a heathen village, and found there one who had been crippled from his birth. He had never walked, or run, or played games, or jumped, or climbed, or done any of the other things boys get up to. He was, and always had been, lame. The little man spoke to him and to others about Jesus, and the cripple listened intently. Suddenly, raising that squeaky voice to a command, the little man told the cripple to stand up – and he did! And walked!

Immediately the whole sleepy village became excited. People ran from every direction, some bearing flowers to decorate the little man, others bringing sacrifices and gifts to offer to him as though he and his companions were gods. One of the companions they called Jupiter, because a temple of Jupiter stood outside the village, and the people seemed to think their own god had come to work miracles among them. The little man, so unhandsome and unimpressive, they called Mercury: because the little man was the chief speaker among the visitors, and Mercury was supposed to be the message-bearer of the gods. Even the priest of the temple of Jupiter joined in the homage to the wonder-working visitors. Everyone had known the lame man for years, ever since they could remember: and now, there he was standing up, walking, running, dancing about in glee. Of course it was a miracle, and these who looked like men must be gods in disguise.

Now that was awkward. The visitors were Christians, and

147

did not believe in these many gods of the heathens. But at first they did not understand what the people were saying, or what was going on. They all spoke in the language of Lycaonia – which the newcomers did not understand. As soon as they realised about the garlands and the gifts and sacrifices, and what it meant, they were horrified. At once they ran in among the crowd, tearing their clothes as a sign of great distress, calling out to people to stop this fuss, and shouting 'We are just men like you! We are just men like you! We bring you good news, that you should turn from these vain gods to the living God, who made the heaven and the earth and the sea and all that is in them. In the past he let all nations walk in their own ways, though he did not leave himself unknown, for he did good, and gave you from heaven rains and fruitful seasons, filling your hearts with food and gladness.'

Crowds change their moods very quickly, and from being excited and grateful, the villagers became sullen and suspicious. No one likes being told his gods are 'vain', or to have his gifts refused. They were offended. Unfortunately, just then some other people arrived, who had pursued the little man from another town that he had visited, where there had been some trouble. These new visitors spread lies about the little man, and the villagers, because they were already offended, were very ready to believe them.

So the mood changed to anger. One after another shouted abuse, calling him names, telling him to go away. (The miracle, and the healed man, were now quite forgotten!) Then someone stupidly threw a stone, then another, and another, then several joined in, and then the whole crowd, until the little man stumbled and fell and lay still. Thinking he was dead, the crowd of course suddenly felt afraid. Each one of them protested 'I did not do it, I did not do it', and the crowd melted away. The little man lay still.

His few companions gathered sadly round him: but they noticed suddenly that he still breathed. Gently they helped him to his feet, and took him to shelter, attended his wounds where the stones had struck him, and made him rest a little.

It was a terrible experience. It showed plainly how very dangerous was this work of preaching the Lord Jesus in heathen lands. It seemed surely a sign from God himself, that they should give up and go home, where at any rate they might not be lied about, and stoned, and left for dead. But the little man would have none of that. He took one night's rest, and went on to the next place, *and began again.*

That was the first New Testament story I can remember hearing. For the little man was Paul: the description of him comes from something written about him quite near his own lifetime; and the story itself from Luke's Book of Acts of the Apostles. I can remember too my own feelings as I listened, or a little of them. For I, too, was small, and not at all good-looking! I was also, probably, something of a coward – at least, I was timid (which sounds better), and very easily frightened and discouraged.

Yet here was a man with few advantages of size, or strength, or appearance, one of a widely disliked and even despised race, preaching a new and daring faith in the God who truly had 'come down to earth'. And in the face of violent attack, and near death, *he just would not be beaten.*

That was the first time I realised that courage is not a matter of being big and strong and bullying. And the first time I began to admire something I have always called bounceback-ability, though the proper word is resilience, or invincibility, or determination or grit. Anyhow, it is the ability to come bouncing back after apparent defeat, undaunted, undismayed, never giving up.

I did not become a Christian for some years after that, but I did learn that Sunday afternoon one thing that led me on to following Christ. I learned that being a Christian might be dangerous and costly, but faith in Christ gave you power to put up with that.

Paul himself wrote some time afterwards, of our being 'more than conquerors' in face of tribulation, hunger, peril and the rest. What he meant by '*more* than conquerors', he himself explains: it means being persecuted, in danger, suffering, frightened, yet never giving up, never becoming separated from the love of God in Christ. It means picking yourself up and going on – sure that God is still with you. I know nothing else in all the world that can give that kind of courage, but faith in the Lord Jesus.

41 He Grew Up

It is strange how some people are never allowed to grow up.
We think of them as children all their lives, in a Peter Pan sort
of way. Everyone talks about 'young Timothy', Paul's assis-
tant, though even by the time Paul had him running all over
the Roman empire on errands, Timothy must have grown a
bit. So too everyone remembers the story of Samuel's childhood, and nearly everyone goes on thinking of Samuel as a
child (and usually in a white nightshirt, too!).

> Hushed was the evening hymn,
>   The temple courts were dark;
> The lamp was burning dim
>   Before the sacred ark,
> When suddenly a voice divine
> Rang through the silence of the shrine.

> The old man, meek and mild,
>   The priest of Israel, slept;
> His watch the temple child,
>   The little Levite kept;
> And what from Eli's sense was sealed
> The Lord to Hannah's son revealed.

Well, yes, it's very nice: but 'the little Levite' was probably
well into his teens, if not late in his twenties, by the time God
called him to be a prophet.

For all that, the early stories of Samuel are worth remembering again: how Hannah, his mother, had longed for a child,
but had none; how she came up year after year to the temple
of God at Shiloh, and often prayed there, privately and
silently, about her longing, and promised that if God would
give her a son, he should be given back to God's service as a
'dedicated man'. And how old Eli, the priest at Shiloh, seeing

her lips moving, thought she was muttering to herself in drunkenness, and rebuked her; and how when she explained, Eli promised that her prayer would be answered.

And so it was, and in due time Hannah fulfilled her promise too, and gave Samuel back to the work of God, first as an attendant on Eli and a servant in the temple. Samuel's mother continued her visits to the temple, bringing Samuel clothes and gifts. What happy reunions those meetings of mother and son must have been, year by year!

But Eli was old, and his sons, who should have followed him in the priesthood, were unworthy men. So it was that God called Samuel, in the night, three times, but Samuel thought it was Eli calling for him. When he went up to Eli the third time, the old man understood what was happening, and advised Samuel how to reply to God. Then God told Samuel that he was to be priest after Eli, instead of Eli's sons. Of course, Eli wanted to know what God had said, and under some pressure Samuel told Eli all about it. The old man took it very well. 'It is the Lord,' he said, 'let him do what seems good to him.'

Yes, it is a good story. But Samuel did grow up, and he became a mighty leader among his people. In days of danger he encouraged and upheld the people in war against the raiding Philistines, always first leading the people in prayer and sacrifice, that they might remember at all times that without God's blessing they would achieve no success.

Samuel became also a 'prophet', which in his case meant two things. People believed that he knew God's secrets, and so could answer their questions, and could find things that were lost. That is why Saul went to Samuel for help, when he was searching for his father's lost asses. They believed, too, that Samuel knew secrets of the future, and could forecast what would happen. But secondly, people believed that Samuel knew God's will, and could teach them God's ways. So Samuel went about the great shrines where Israel gathered at festival times to worship, and there he taught the people the truth, and the ways of God.

As if that was not enough, Samuel was also consulted very often by people who had complaints against their neighbours and wanted things put right; or by people who were arguing about who owned property, or about some old quarrel, and who asked Samuel to hear both sides and settle who was right. So Samuel became a 'judge' over Israel, wise, trusted, and faithful to God's law: a great man indeed.

And then he became more again. The people of Israel looked at their neighbours, the other nations round about them, and saw that they had splendid kings, wealthy and powerful and very proud. So, Israel wanted a king too. Samuel told them that God was their king, but that did not satisfy them. Then Samuel told them how a king would make them pay taxes, would take their sons to be soldiers and their daughters to be pastrycooks and maid-servants, and how they would regret having a king when they had to pay for him and do what they were told. But it was no use: still the people insisted, not really believing what Samuel said.

So Samuel prayed about it, and with God guiding him he chose as the first king of Israel the tall and handsome Saul. When Saul was crowned, Samuel set down in a book the way the kingdom should be governed, and the laws of God that even the king had to obey, lest Saul should become too big for his shoes and begin to misuse his power.

Several times Samuel, on behalf of the people, and in God's name, needed to rebuke Saul for disobeying God, or for trying to take the priests' place, but he was never afraid to do so. Eventually, when Saul failed in the great opportunity which God had given him, it was Samuel who saved the people from a disastrous war among themselves, by choosing young David to be the next king and anointing him in preparation for taking Saul's place. That was an exceedingly dangerous thing to do while Saul still ruled, but how right that choice proved to be, and how wise was the foresight which had a new king in readiness.

Add all that up – leader and encourager in dark days, finder of lost things and counsellor of the people, judge in disputes and teacher of God's laws, twice a king-maker and a defender of the people's rights, and of God's, when the king got out of hand – and you can see why we should remember that 'the little Levite' grew into one of the finest of Israel's heroes. But among all that we admire in Samuel, I think it is his *loyalty* that I count greatest. Think of it.

152

When old Eli's family was rejected from the priesthood, Samuel out of loyalty did not want to tell him so; and – again out of loyalty – continued to serve Eli faithfully until God removed him. When the people clamoured for a king, wrongly as Samuel thought, he still continued faithfully to intercede for them, saying 'God forbid that I should sin against the Lord in ceasing to pray for you'. And when Saul had to be told that God was taking the kingship away from him, and Saul in his shame and grief pleaded that nevertheless Samuel would honour him before the elders of Israel and join him in worshipping God, Samuel agreed to do so. Again out of loyalty, he faithfully supported Saul until God should in his own time remove him. It takes a very big man to stand by people he does not fully agree with, and remain faithful to those whom he thinks God will remove.

That kind of loyalty is very rare. It is completely selfless – Samuel after all could himself have been king without much trouble, had he wished. And it is completely reliable: Eli, Saul, people in trouble, the nation as a whole, all knew they could count on Samuel to do right, whatever happened. And so could God: for Samuel was above all a faithful servant of God.

No wonder that, when he died all Israel assembled and mourned for him.

42 At the Sign of a Christian

Shop signs are among the oldest street decorations in the world. Long before most people could read 'Jones and Son, Butchers' over the door, or 'Woolworths', or 'Post Office', people doing business and eager to attract customers hung out painted signs to show what goods they sold, what service they offered. A wine-seller might hang a wine barrel high above his doorway; a barber used a striped pole to advertise his trade; the money-lender fastened three golden balls above his shop.

Sometimes the business man copied his sign also on a metal or jewelled seal, with which he 'signed' his name on letters, receipts and documents. The symbol was cut into the signet ('sign it') ring worn upon his finger, and would be pressed onto hot wax and held until it cooled. Such a sign would then prove who had 'signed and sealed' the letter or document.

All this once troubled a great Christian leader, long ago in Egypt. His name was Clement, and he was the revered teacher and pastor of many living in the great business centre and seaport of Alexandria. What bothered Clement as he went about his pastoral visiting was that Christian business men used the same signs, and the same symbolic signet rings, as other people did. Some of these were pictures and carvings of pagan gods and goddesses: the wine-seller might hang a painting of the god of wine above his door, and so on. Other signs were daggers, swords, axes, winecups, dice, and things of that kind. This is all wrong, Clement thought: Christians are not idolators, nor fighters and brawlers, nor drunkards and gamblers. They are a different sort of people altogether, and they should show it by using entirely different signs. Let them advertise their business in a Christian way, and they will advertise Christianity too.

So Clement advised what the signs of the Christians ought to be. The dove descending from the sky should show the Christian as one who had followed Jesus in his baptism, when the Holy Spirit descended in the form of a dove and rested upon him. A ship with all her sails spread and filled out with a strong wind should be the sign of those who had found the Ark of Salvation by believing in Jesus. Both these signs are still used by Christians in every land to this day.

Clement also asked the ship-owners at Alexandria to look again at their great vessels, riding at anchor in the bay, or putting out grandly to sea on the long journey with wheat to Rome: and to notice high above each prow the yard-arm carrying the foremost sail crossing the high proud foremast, forming the sign of the cross. 'That', said Clement, 'shall be your sign – let it always keep you in mind of the death of your Saviour!'

If too many wanted to use that sign for their trade, let others copy on their seals the sign of the anchor, to show they had come safe through every storm to anchor their trust in the safe refuge, the Lord Jesus.

Such a good idea soon caught on. Christian signs, with lovely meanings, began to be found everywhere, in the meeting places, decorating Christian churches, and wistfully distinguishing Christian graves. A palm branch was the sign of peace; a star the symbol of hope. A young deer, or hart, panting for the cooling stream of baptism symbolised the new convert. The letters IHS stood for Jesus, either as the first three letters of his (Greek) name, or as meaning (in Latin) 'Jesus, the Saviour of men'. Once the symbol became widely used, it seems likely that Greeks explained it one way and Latin-speaking Christians explained it the other way.

Two other letters, A and Z, were used to show that Jesus is the beginning and the end of Christian faith. A vine with many branches recalled the words of Jesus about abiding in him if we would bear fruit. A three-leaved shamrock was used to suggest how Christians thought of God, as Father, Son, and Holy Spirit.

In time, many hundreds of such signs were invented and loved by Christians everywhere. It is interesting to walk around an old church even yet looking for such things. Above all, and more than all, the sign of the cross showed where Christians worshipped, lived, worked, and were buried. Explaining the signs to interested enquirers gave many opportunities to preach the gospel to new people.

But of course there are other signs by which the Christian can be known. In the middle ages, Peter Cerano was cast upon a deserted island, all alone, when his small ship went down in a storm. On that island he lived for seven years, barely keeping himself alive. When he had almost despaired of ever being rescued, a ship appeared, and he went wild with joy, shouting, crying, leaping and waving his arms. Curious, a few sailors set out in a small boat, to investigate what was happening on the island, but as they drew near, they saw the shouting leaping man, with hair down to his elbows, and a beard down to his knees, almost black from the sun, and deliriously happy – they thought he was mad. Wouldn't you? So they began to turn the boat and hastily row away.

What could he do, to convince them he was not a savage, or mad, but perfectly sane and civilised? Brilliantly, he hit upon something that had been his comfort and strength through the long years. He began to shout –

> I BELIEVE in God, the Father almighty, Maker of heaven and earth
> And in Jesus Christ his only Son, our Lord, who was conceived by the Holy Ghost, born of the Virgin Mary . . .

and so on, through the Apostles' Creed, which was recited, at that time in the same language, in churches all over Europe and beyond. At once the sailors knew that he was sane, and civilised, and Christian, and turned back for him. So the Christian is known, in all kinds of strange places and company, by the great things he *believes*.

And Jesus himself gave us another sign, perhaps the most important of all: 'Love one another: by this shall all men know that you are my disciples.'

Hoist your signals, and let your friends know what you are!

43 The Fish

Two friends were being carried in a litter through the streets of ancient Rome. One, a young man, was telling the other of the wonderful girl he had met, and how he had fallen deeply in love. The older man was envious, and questioned him about her; had he spoken to the girl? what did she say?

'She was uneasy,' the younger man replied, 'and listened to me with bended head, while she traced some lines on the yellow sand with a reed. Then she raised her eyes, looked down again at the figure she had traced, lifted them once more to me as though she would ask me a question, and suddenly ran away like a nymph from a stupid faun.'

'What did she trace on the sand?'

'A fish.'

'A *what*?'

'A fish, I tell you. Did that mean that the blood in her veins was cold? I've no idea. But please interpret it for me.'

'My dear fellow, you'll have to ask Pliny; he's the man who knows about fish.'

There the conversation rested, for now the litter was passing through the crowded streets ...

A little later, a Roman official is questioning someone about the escape of the same girl from capture; a rascal called Chilon replies:

'... The maiden is certainly a worshipper of the same deity as Pomponia, most virtuous of Roman women ... I could not learn from her people what deity it was, or the name of those who worshipped it. If I could find that out, I'd go to them and become the most pious of disciples, and so win their confidence. But you, sir . . . can you throw some light on the matter?

'No,' said Vinicius.

'Well, you have questioned me about all sorts of things, noble sirs,' said the rascal, 'and I have answered your question. Allow me now in my turn to put a few to you. Illustrious tribune, did you never notice any ceremony, or anything connected with their worship, a statuette, perhaps, or a sacrifice, or an amulet? Did you never observe them drawing any symbols only Pomponia and the young foreign girl could understand?

'Symbols? Wait now! Yes! One day I saw Lygia trace a fish on the sand.'

'A fish? Oh! Indeed! Only once, or more than once?'

'Once.'

'And are you sure, sir, that she traced a – a *fish*? Oh!'

'Yes,' said Vinicius, becoming curious. 'Do you know what it means?'

'Know what it means!' exclaimed Chilon. Then, with a bow he added, 'May Fortune ever load you with her favours . . .' and went off muttering evilly to himself, 'Oh, she traced a fish on the sand, did she? If I know what that means, may I choke on my next mouthful of goat cheese! But I'll get to know . . .'

A little later Chilon is sitting in a tavern, arguing with the landlord about the quality of the wine, and suddenly he dips his finger in his glass and drew a fish on the table-top.

'Do you know what that means?' he asked.

'A fish? What a question. A fish – it's a fish!'

'And you – you're an ass . . .' Chilon answered rudely, and went off to enquire elsewhere.

Later again, Chilon returned to Vinicius, saying 'The first time, sir, I brought you hope; now I bring you the assurance that the girl will be found.'

'And that means that you have not found her yet?'

'It does, sir. But I have found out the meaning of the symbol which she traced for you; I know who the people are who have taken her away, and I know what god it is they worship.'

Vinicius would have started from his seat, but Petronius (his friend) laid his hand on his shoulder and said:

'Go on.'

'Are you perfectly sure, sir, that the maiden traced a fish on the sand?'

'Yes.'

'Then she is a Christian, and it is the Christians who have her.' (Petronius and Vinicius find this hard to believe, and doubt the word of Chilon. They have many reasons why, as they think, so lovely a lady would never join the Christians. But Chilon insists, and when the two friends ask his reasons, he goes on,)

'Repeat this phrase in Greek, sir: Jesus Christ, Son of God, Saviour.'

(Petronius did so, adding) 'Well, there you are. What now?'

'Now take the first letter of each of these words and join the letters so as to make a new word.'

'Fish!' exlaimed Petronius, in astonishment.

'That's why the fish is the emblem of Christianity,' Chilon replied proudly.

Asked to explain how he had found this out, Chilon tells how he had walked the streets of Rome, visiting taverns, bakehouses, butchers, fish sellers, olive sellers, laundries, cookshops, muleteers, stone-carvers, dentists, merchants and hosts of others (Chilon hopes to be well paid, so he exaggerated his toil!), making people talk to him. As they talked, Chilon had drawn a fish in front of them, and watched for some reaction. Nothing happened, he said, until he found an old slave by a fountain, weeping. Chilon drew the sad story out of the slave, of how he had gone to great lengths in order to buy his own son into freedom, but the slave master had taken the money (which the slave ought not to have) and kept the boy. Chilon pretended great sympathy with the old man, and as he offered comfort, dipped his hand in the fountain and drew a fish on the stones. Immediately, the old slave said, 'My trust is also in the Christ.' Chilon had replied, 'You recognised me by this sign?' And the slave answered, 'Yes. Peace be with you.'

All that comes from one of the greatest stories ever written about the early Christians. It is called *Quo Vadis*, and was written by Henryk Sienkiewicz (don't try to say it, just sneeze!). Although it is a story, it is based on truth, and you may accept what Chilon says about the meaning of the fish sign, although he was a treacherous rascal.

Here is wisdom, and mystery, and secret meanings! Of course the first disciples were fishermen, and Jesus had said, 'Follow me, and I will make you fishers of men.' But the real meaning of the fish sign is just as Chilon said: in Greek,

I may stand for *Jesus* (I and J are the same letter in Greek)
CH may stand for *Christ*
TH may stand for *of God* (theou)
U may stand for *Son* (uios)
S may stand for *Saviour* (soter)

and ICHTHUS means 'fish' – or, Jesus Christ, Son of God, Saviour.

So when any man, in strange company, made the sign of the fish in sand, or on a wall, or doodling with his pen, he was saying to anyone able to understand (as a fellow Christian would), 'I believe in Jesus Christ, the Son of God, the Saviour.' And so Christian recognised Christian, without their enemies knowing. The fish sign was more secret than the cross sign, and it became almost as famous as the symbol of a Christian.

Why not make yourself a little fish, wear it on your coat, learn *exactly* what it means, and be ready to explain it to your friends?

44 Cryptograms

Behind me as I write this story there hangs on my study wall a green card, to which is fixed what looks like a thin piece of stone, flat, light brown in colour, and bearing curious marks that have a hidden meaning. They are cryptograms, or code-signs.

There are two fishes, which at once tell you what this is all about, for these are the early Christian symbols of *Christians*. But these are funny little fish: whoever scratched them on the stone would never get full marks at school for drawing.

And these fish look as though they have been caught, by nibbling at the two ends of a large anchor – another Christian sign, as you will remember. Then there is a strange little figure like a match-stick man, with straight legs and back-bone, but with a circle for his body, and what seem to be match-stick arms straight out from his shoulders and slightly raised. This, almost certainly, is the symbol of the man at prayer, a reminder of the need of prayer found in many ancient places.

Beside this again is a drawing which quite baffles everyone. It is a vertical line, with a small circle at the top; two circles, one inside the other, at the centre; and a small circle at the bottom. Your guess as to its meaning is as likely to be right as anyone else's, so draw it, and think it over. It is just possible that the diagram symbolizes the Lord's Supper, two fishes, or two winecups, and between them a loaf upon a plate: no one can be sure.

Mine is a plaster imitation of a real piece of stone from ancient Rome. The story behind it is very interesting. The Romans buried their dead always outside the walls of their city, usually in underground caves and tunnels linked by miles of corridors cut in the soft stone of the Roman hills. Here bodies were laid on stone shelves, with sweet herbs and flowers, and carvings, inscriptions and paintings marked the

F

place of people dearly loved, or held to be of great importance.

Some lovely pictures can still be seen in these underground caverns. One shows Love and Psyche (the soul) picking flowers apparently in the gardens of 'heaven'; another, above a Jewish grave, shows David and his sling; yet another shows the little girl (Ciriaca) who had died, running joyfully after her hoop as she used to do, though now in the picture a tree shows she is running in the fields of heaven and not the city streets.

The Roman people thought of burial places as especially sacred, and would allow no plundering or violence near them. So when later on Christians began to be persecuted for their faith and forbidden to worship or to preach the gospel, they often sought refuge in these caverns and tunnels, where no one would pursue them. There they often gathered for worship; there they sometimes hid themselves in times of peril; there they eventually came to bury their own dead. They showed especial reverence and care towards the bodies of those who had died in the Roman arena, or in the streets, for

their faith, and there were many of these, for Rome put many Christians to death.

And so the 'catacombs', as these hallowed places are called, came to be decorated also with Christian paintings, sculptures and inscriptions, and from them we can still learn much of how Christians thought and felt in those far off, dangerous days. A butterfly often symbolises the Christian soul fluttering off happily to heaven. A peacock, or a phoenix (a fabled bird, supposed to hatch out its one and only egg in the flames of its own nest, in which it perished) became the symbol of the Christian rising from the dead. Here and there a joyful harvest scene suggests the reward which the Christian may expect in heaven for his work on earth. Everywhere is the figure of the Good Shepherd, leading his sheep to eternal life. Those early Christians, face to face so often with death, do not seem to have been afraid, but rather to have been sure of life ever-lasting.

One especially beautiful communion cup found in the cata-combs has on it this figure of the Good Shepherd, but on his shoulders he is carrying not a lost sheep, which everyone after all loves or pities, but a smelly, heavy, ill-tempered *goat*, the symbol of sinners, whom no one except the Good Shepherd ever loves, or pities. Whoever made and painted that cup had thought a lot about the gospel!

Just who my copied piece of stone commemorated, I cannot say; the name has been broken off. Could the *two* fishes repre-sent brothers, or sisters, or even (I like to think) twins, who were 'anchored' in Christ? Does the prayer-symbol mean that they were noted for their prayerfulness? or does it mean their parents will continue to pray for them? And does the symbol of the Lord's Supper (if that is what it is) mean that they were members of the church, who will be missed at the Lord's Table? We wish we knew more.

But puzzling though the details are, I like to glance some-times at my little plaque, and remember the hosts of brave and good people, young and old, who lived and died for Christ all those years ago in ancient Rome.

45 Four Reporters

There was great excitement in our village one Friday morning. The local timber-yard caught fire. What a blaze! And what a fuss! No one was hurt, so all the boys and girls could enjoy the fun without regrets.

Until, that is, the Fire Brigade arrived, or nearly arrived. For the fire engine overturned at a large roundabout in the centre of the village, and some firemen were hurt, but not very badly.

As so often, I missed all the excitement, only hearing about it afterwards: but that too was interesting. For one boy stopped me in the road to say something like: 'Ooh! You should have seen it, Mr White. The fire engine came zooming up the main road, grrr, grrr, grrr, with the bell janglangling, and zooming round the bend at sixty, and suddenly there was a most awful crash, and there it was all smashed on its side and the paint scratched and a wheel off, and the engine part went on racing, it was marvellous, and the wood blazing all the time – you *should* have seen it!' (Even my ears were out of breath, but I felt I almost had seen it, through his eyes.)

Another youngster, a girl, described it to me quite differently a little later. She was there, too, but she saw (or at any rate, she remembered) only the hurt men lying by the road until an ambulance came, the bandages, and the blood on the grass; and she told me in a whisper how one of the men moaned and moaned. 'It was terrible, terrible,' she said, still very upset.

In the evening a young man told me the engine was doing about thirty-two to thirty-five as it approached the crossing; the driver, he said, did not seem to be sure which road led to the timber-yard, so he did not get into the right position on the road; in the end he took the bend a shade too close to the curb. His one back wheel mounted the curb and the grass slope, so of course over he went.

The next day, someone said to me, 'It's too bad, really. Since the village became part of B—— we have to wait for the Brigade, and the ambulances, and everything else, to come from the Town Centre; of course, that takes time, and everything is done in a rush, by men who do not know all the local conditions. We must press to have a fire engine kept nearer the village. If we organised properly, such accidents as yesterday's need never happen.'

One only saw it, and was excited; one felt, and was upset; one described what happened, calmly and exactly; and one had thought about it very carefully, and about what could be done to prevent such things. Yet they were all reporting the same event. None of us can help it: we all see things with our own eyes, our own minds, and our own hearts; and not one of us, however clever or careful we try to be, ever sees the *whole* truth about anything.

I was reminded of an old eastern tale, of four blind men taken to 'see' an elephant for the first time. The first man's hands discovered the elephant's trunk, and felt it over carefully. 'I know what an elephant is like,' he said, 'it's like a long, thin snake.' The second man found the animal's huge leg, and put his arms around it. 'Nonsense,' he said to the first man, 'an elephant is like a strong, straight tree.'

But the third man had reached up to the elephant's ear, and exploring it sensitively with his fingers, he said, 'I do not understand what you two mean: the elephant is a big leather bird.' The fourth man was stroking the huge curved tusk. 'Snake? Tree? Bird?' he said, 'Nonsense, all of you. The elephant is made of marble.'

Describing the same creature, each honestly trying to get it right; each actually right, in his own way; yet so different!

Is it not wonderful that God arranged for us to have *four* stories of Jesus? Not just one, but four Gospels, each looking at Jesus in a particular way, so that we can put them together, and see him clearly and understand him better.

Mark saw what happened, and tells it excitedly, in a rush. *Luke* saw Jesus especially as the Friend of sinners, the sick, the lost and the lonely, and he makes us feel the love of Jesus. *Matthew* thinks out what he counts most important, gives much more space to the teaching of Jesus, and how all he did and said fulfilled the scriptures. *John* thought long and deeply about the story, and tells us what it all means – that 'if we believe in Jesus, and trust him as Lord and Saviour, we have eternal life'.

Every true story is better told if more than one contributes to the telling: 'in the mouths of two, or three, witnesses every word shall be established.' More surely still with four.

46 Christians at Work

Fifteen-years-old Moon Pyung Chan longed to possess a Bible of his own. He could just read, but he had no books at all. Nor did he think about having other books – it was a Bible he wanted.

But he was an 'unpaid' scholar even in school – which meant that his parents could not pay for his place in class. He had been given a place, but the school could not afford to give him books, or pens, or the special clothes for sport and drill, or anything else. How could school, or his home, afford to give him a Bible? Yet he sorely wanted one, so that he could read the Jesus-stories at home, and in bed.

Then one Sunday in church, the minister announced that men from the Bible printers – the Bible Society, he called it – were to come to the village shortly, with lots of copies of the scriptures. That made Chan feel even sadder, until the minister added that the Bible men would accept whatever people could give – farm produce, fruit, rice-crops, beans, chestnuts, potatoes, carved things – in exchange for the scriptures.

That put an idea in Chan's head. He knew where there was lots of rice-straw, the stalks of the rice left over when the rice-grains had been removed. When the right time came, it would be burned, anyway, and no one would mind if he took some. As soon as he got home he began to collect longer stalks of straw, and he knew well how to plait them into strong rope. He was not sure when the Bible-men would come, or how much was needed. So he began early each morning, before work and school, and he went on late into each night. But he was very happy – he felt that a Bible was indeed within reach at last, and how proud he would be of it; how he would enjoy reading the bits he already knew, and other parts he knew nothing about.

By the time the Bible-men with their van arrived at the village, Chan had a great pile of rice-straw-rope all ready. As soon as he could, when the van stopped beside the Church, Chan gathered up his rope in a huge bundle in his arms – it was very light, but it made a great pile high above his head, so that he had to look *round* it to see where he was going. The report says that when they measured it out, there were four hundred and fifty-five feet of good rice-straw-rope! Chan received a new, shining-covered, New Testament. He ran home clutching it tightly, eyes shining, tears running down his face, and a broad smile from ear to ear.

(A New Testament for four hundred and fifty-five feet! If I were making up this story, I would have said that Chan received a Bible. But I must keep to the truth. Besides I can remember straw-ropes – they are not very strong, and they rotted very quickly, so perhaps even long ones were not worth very much. Anyway, Chan was absolutely delighted, and he should know! I feel sure he got a whole Bible eventually.)

But here is a sad, and shocking, story.

Lee Jae Ku was a much smaller boy, and much poorer. He had no home at all, no parents, no bed, nothing. He scrambled about the streets of Taejon, in Korea, shivering, begging from passers-by, searching the rubbish-cans behind shops and cafés for scraps of stale food. In summer it was bad enough, in winter – terrible. He spent weeks hungry, wet and cold.

But one winter was worse than ever, and his bare feet actually froze upon the pavement. He lay helpless, in intense pain, until a policeman found him. Then he was taken into a hospital – such as it was, under-staffed, with few of the drugs and instruments hospitals ought to have, and no money to get them. Still, he was indoors, and there was some food. Then the first blow fell.

His feet were so badly frozen that they had to be cut off. It was the only way to save his life. It was expertly and kindly done, but then there were so few to care for all the patients, and Ku lay waiting for his legs to heal, with only occasional attention, and no one to comfort him, for a long time. It was spring before he was anything like well. Then the second dreadful blow fell.

Ku was carried from his hospital bed, his poor legs unbandaged now, and laid upon the pavement where he had been found. It was wet and muddy after a day's rain; but there he lay. Neither the nurses, nor the hospital, nor anyone else, was responsible for him, or had enough to share with all the poor of Taejon. The medical job was done: now he must fend for himself. But he could no longer stand and beg, nor could he go from rubbish-can to yard hunting for scraps. All he could do was to crawl slowly for a little way at a time, and grow hungrier.

Ku did that for two days, then it appears that he fainted from exhaustion and pain.

Suddenly, a lady was bending over him. She moved him into a more comfortable position, then began asking kindly, gentle questions – who was he, where was his home, who looked after him then, and so on. When the real position was clear, she beckoned to a driver nearby, and – strangest wonder in the world! – a motor truck came up, with benches and seats fixed in the back, and Ku was lifted into it. There he found a number of people of varying ages – *and all had feet, or hands, or arms, missing.* Except for the lady and the driver, Ku was the same as everyone present! – a bit younger than anyone else, and thinner, and certainly dirtier: but his injury was in a sense no longer something to hide, or for others to laugh at, but shared. Not even in the hospital had Ku seen anything like this.

He was taken in the truck, amidst many more questions, much sympathy, and great friendliness, to a very special clinic, set up by missionaries for war-wounded people and anyone else who had lost arms or feet or hands. The idea was to help such people to work for themselves, and so rescue them from poverty and wretchedness. The clinic specialises in artificial hands and arms, legs and feet, made with un-believable cleverness; and patients are taught again to use these as 'tools' (so to speak) in earning their own livelihood.

Ku was first given – a warm bath! Then a suit of comfortable clothes. Then food – as much as he wanted. Then he was taken round the clinic and shown other boys, and girls, and men and women, doing remarkably well with artificial limbs in place of those they had lost. And he was promised new feet, and training, and school, and a place to live and be cared for, until he could manage alone. It took him a long time to take it all in – longer still to believe it! But the gentleness, the friend-liness, the happiness around him, began to melt his cold little heart. And soon he began to hear why the missionaries were doing all this – for love of Jesus, and of those whom Jesus loves.

Between them Moon Pyung Chan and Lee Jae Ku illus-trate the two chief tasks of Christian missionaries, in every part of the world. To *teach* the word of God's great love, and to *show* the depth of God's great love, in every land.

Would you not like to join them?

47 Handicapped, but Helped

We all feel sorry for handicapped people, or we ought to; for those who are invalid, or blind, or lame, or deaf; those who never had opportunity for education; who never knew a loving family and a good, comfortable home; those deformed from birth, or permanently injured by accident, or by war. There are so many such folk around us all, and to feel sorry is the first, most natural response to them – though it is never enough; *feeling* sorry is mere pretence if it does not make us *act* kindly.

But so often we have to *admire* handicapped people, too. They are, more often than not, extremely brave, remarkably clever, and wonderfully patient. Probably you know a number of people like that, as I certainly do. But, to avoid being personal and rude, let us think instead of a few outstanding cases, whose courage became famous.

A Greek boy of long ago, named Demosthenes, came to be held up as an example to every Greek (and Roman, I suspect) who grumbled about being handicapped. When Demosthenes was only seven his father died; and when he was eighteen, he found that his guardians, who should have looked after his father's property for him and educated him and his younger sister, had in fact squandered everything, leaving them both very poor. Demosthenes, very daringly, appeared before a judge in the court to accuse the guardians. Everyone advised him not to do this, since he would have nothing to pay for a lawyer to plead for him, and the judge would only laugh at him. However, he persisted, the judge was kind, and the guardians were ordered to restore the lost fortune.

This experience made Demosthenes decide to become a public speaker, and plead for other people before the courts – whether they could pay or not. The Greeks thought that to be such an orator was one of the greatest careers a man could choose – rather as we think of sportsmen, film-stars, singers, musicians, surgeons, in our day.

But there arose the difficulty, in fact several difficulties. In the first place, Demosthenes could not speak clearly. Some say he could not pronounce his 'R's' properly, so that people laughed at him. Most say that he stammered. For a second thing, he had poor lungs, and soon lost his breath if he exerted himself at all. For a third thing, his voice was not good, being rather high-pitched and weak: he could not easily be heard unless you stood near him. And in the fourth place, a nervous twitch kept shrugging his shoulder, so that he was most irritating for any audience to watch.

So much for handicaps. And he wanted to be a public orator!

But Demosthenes had decided, and so he set about it. First he confided in a friend, who was himself an excellent speaker, and together they got down to this difficulty of pronouncing words. It was hard work, with many hours of boring practice, but Demosthenes kept at it, curing himself of one fault, then another, and then another, month after month, year after year. To strengthen his breathing, he used every day to run uphill while reciting poetry aloud. That was a trying business; he often felt ill and exhausted; many advised him to give up. But he persisted.

To develop a strong voice, that could shout down hecklers and interruptions in court, and keep going for a long time, Demosthenes practised speeches on the seashore, making himself heard above the rush and clamour of the waves. While to overcome his twitching shoulder, he actually used to sit in his room in a straight chair, with a sharp sword so fixed that every time he shrugged the point pierced his skin!

It took ten years: but when he was thirty, Demosthenes began to gain a wide reputation as a public speaker, and after his death he was acclaimed as the greatest orator in all Greece – that country of fine speakers. Demosthenes himself used to say that his success was due to the encouragement he received: 'I had a friend' he used to say. We might add, that he had a fine, unselfish motive – to speak up well for other people. Those two together can overcome most handicaps.

William Lloyd Garrison has a special place in American

history. There were many who were disturbed about the practice of slavery, and many brave things were done, brave voices were raised, in the long struggle to abolish the system altogether. But most of the very bravest would agree that the *pioneer*, the man who first awakened many consciences, the one who framed the strongest arguments, appealed most persuasively to the compassion of ordinary people, was William Lloyd Garrison.

Once such a movement for reform has started, and gained money, influence, support, much of the danger decreases, and hard work will see it done. But at the beginning, when only one or two are pressing new, unwelcome ideas on the public mind, it can be very dangerous to demand changes. The slave-owners, the slave-masters, the owners of the ships who brought the slaves, the business men who made much money out of slavery – all these, and many, many more, were ready to silence any protests, to ridicule the arguments brought against their trade, and if none of this succeeded, then they threatened the opponents of slavery with all kinds of trouble. They were sacked from their work, sometimes they were refused employment; their houses were burned down; a few were killed. It was a bitter struggle, and bitterest of all for the pioneers, the brave few who believed it was wrong, and said so.

The pioneer himself, William Lloyd Garrison, had nothing to fight with. He had no money, to take enemies to court, or to advertise, or to pay for helpers. He had no friends, either, at the start, for most thought him a fanatic, half-mad. He had not much education – not such as the slave-owners could command in speakers and lawyers. No one at first even knew who he was, for he had no public position or fame. He was only a poor printer.

Yet in the end he won through. The movement for abolishing slavery through America gathered support and grew quite rapidly, until powerful people joined in, and the Abolition Law was passed. Then people looked back with wonder to the young man who had begun it all, handicapped by so many disadvantages. And an American poet spoke the admiration of thousands –

In a small chamber, friendless and alone
    Toiled o'er his types one poor, unlearned young man.
The place was dark, unfurnitured, and mean
    Yet there the freedom of a race began.

Help came but slowly – surely no man yet
    Put lever to the heavy world with less!
What need of help? He knew how types were set,
    He had a dauntless spirit – and a press.

And he too had a fine and selfless motive, to deliver others from bondage and suffering. He was not sorry for himself.

The most famous of all handicapped people of our own time was a girl, her name Helen Keller. She was born in 1880 and lived to be eighty-eight years old. But when she was only a baby she became both blind and deaf. Because this happened before she had learned to speak, Helen was also, for a long time believed to be dumb: certainly she could not make the sounds necessary for talking.

It is quite impossible to imagine what it must be like, to be alive, and feeling things, and wanting things, yet unable to see, or to hear, or to speak. It is nearly as impossible to imagine what you can do for a baby like that: how can you speak, or smile, or become known to the child; how can you teach anything, or begin to train in even the ordinary things babies have to learn? It must have been simply overwhelming in sadness, and helplessness, for Helen's parents.

But a friend comes into this story too, a most devoted, incredibly patient, and very gifted teacher. She was Anne M. Sullivan, later Mrs Macy. She it was who bore all Helen's helplessness, learned how to accept, and when to check, Helen's tantrums and terrible tempers, and finally won the poor child's implicit trust and love. Miss Sullivan, too, accepted the challenge of finding a way to get into touch with Helen's mind, in her darkness and silence. She did it by holding Helen's hand, and touching her separate fingers, in one way for approval, another disapproval; one way for making the right sound, another way when Helen made the wrong sound. This went on for many months – but in the end, triumphantly, Helen was taught to *speak*.

Next came teaching, by the same hand movements, all kinds of things, and the slow work went on all through Helen's growing years. Miss Sullivan must have been one of the world's great teachers, for when Helen was twenty-four, still blind and deaf, she took her University degree. She then became a speaker at public meetings, and so became a noted lecturer in various subjects; and after a while she began to 'write' (dictating what she wanted written), and so became known far beyond America.

Helen Keller's photograph is in front of me now; she looks a very stately, gracious, and above all a *happy* woman. What a magnificent triumph over handicaps!

Her secret, of course, lay in her friend. But I have also in front of me some words she wrote herself: 'Active faith knows no fear, and it is a safeguard to me against cynicism and despair. Belief in God as infinite good Will and all-seeing Wisdom, whose everlasting arms sustain me walking on the sea of life (is part of faith). Fate has its master in the faith of those who surmount it; limitations have their limits for those who live greatly' (remember what her fate, and her limitations, had been).

One other remark she made shows the same unselfishness that we noticed in handicapped Demosthenes and handicapped Garrison. Helen said: 'It was a terrible blow to my faith when I learned that millions of my fellow creatures must labour all their days for food and shelter, bear the most crushing burdens, and die without having known the joy of living. When I think of the suffering and famine, and the continued slaughter of men, my spirit bleeds; but the thought comes to me that, like the little deaf, dumb, and blind child I once was, mankind too is growing out of the darkness of ignorance and hatred, into the light of a brighter day.'

A good friend, an unselfish attitude, and a high faith, can conquer almost any handicap, it seems.

48 How Do You Read?

A very learned man asked Jesus once what he needed to do in order to be sure of receiving eternal life. Jesus answered, 'What is written in the law? How do you read?' After all, the man was a lawyer and should know what God's law said; so why ask Jesus? The man showed at once that he did know: 'You shall love the Lord your God with all your heart, and with all your soul, and with all your strength, and with all your mind; and your neighbour as yourself.' Then Jesus said to him, 'You have answered right; do this, and you will live.' So, the man knew the answer to his own question: what Jesus asked him was, do you understand what you read? and do you really *listen* to what you read, and do it? '*How* do you read?'

I expect you have forgotten now what a business it was learning to read. It is rather like cycling, and swimming: once you have learned, you cannot remember what it was like when you could not do it.

Some African boys were helping to unload a missionary's luggage from the canoe on the river, and to carry it into his house. They were very inquisitive (as all boys are) and they wondered at the strange things the white man had brought with him. Most of them seemed to have no use at all. Then one boy dropped a book on to the table, and it fell open. Immediately two or three boys gathered round and *watched* it. After a moment or two, one of the boys cautiously reached his finger to the page and tried to push the printed letters along, to make them move. Of course nothing happened, and the boys turned away disappointed. 'They're dead' said one of them, and left the book alone.

Since they had never seen print before, they thought the letters were insects, such as could be found crowded on to a leaf in the forest, and which a touch with the finger could send scurrying in all directions! What a job, to start right at the beginning, and teach these lads to read. But the missionary would do it; and African boys are very quick to learn.

'How do you read?' The marks on the paper stand for sounds, and the sounds make words, and the words put together say things, and you listen to yourself saying them, and get the meaning. So by the printed page, someone a thousand miles away has 'talked' to you. If the book was first written a long time ago, perhaps someone who died a long time before you were born has spoken to you through the marks on the page, and you have 'listened' to his words. So you have come to think what he was thinking, long ago . . . Reading *is* wonderful, isn't it? Even the shapes of the letters are fascinating – I wonder who first drew them. Some say A used to represent a camel; B was a house (presumably with the bedroom upstairs); C was a boy with his mouth open . . . It seems hard to believe. But the shapes *are* very, very old: the oldest writing in the world is on a clay tablet found near ancient Babylon. Someone wrote instructions on the soft, moist clay, and set it out in the sun to dry: but before it dried, a dog stepped on it, and there his paw-mark still is, like a blot on the oldest page ever written! That reminds us, reading is important not only

for books, but for street names, our own names, shop names, instructions on packets, and medicines, and 'How to use the Telephone', and thousands of other uses. It is wonderful to be *able* to read, isn't it?

The National Christian Council of India organised night schools where people could learn to read in the scattered villages and towns, after their day's work. To advertise the classes, and encourage the pupils, a great prize-giving was arranged, and people gathered into one large village from twenty miles around to share the excitement. There were reading competitions, letter-writing competitions, word-races, a procession with written banners, singing (from papers!), a film was shown, and there was a feast – with *written* invitations. Fifty new readers, who had learned to read in the past three years, were especially honoured.

Each home was visited, and when someone who could read was found within, a silver star was fixed to the door, one for each reader. What pride families had, in their 'star' readers! Each person who could read was given a red star, too, and these were worn very prominently for days.

One old man had brought his string cot out into the village street, to watch the fun, and half-lay with a child on his lap, enjoying everything. As the home-visitors passed by, the old man stretched out his hand for a star. 'But can *you* read, Grandfather?' they asked, not really believing that he could. 'Yes, I can,' he said, shyly. Still the questioners doubted: 'Well,' they said, 'read us a bit of the Bible.'

But the old man did not have a Bible. 'It is a long time since I had one,' the old man said, 'My son took it away when he went into the town.' Still not quite believing, the visitors sent for a Bible in his language: there was only one in the village, and it belonged to the minister.

The old man opened it, and slowly, stumblingly, began to read, the little child on his knee watching grandfather's bent and bony finger move from word to word. Everyone near fell silent, and the old man became completely absorbed, reading as a thirsty man might drink his first water for days. He forgot the visitors, and the villagers, and the stars, and the fun and commotion – he read on, and on, 'drinking in' the beloved words, page after page.

'It was a long time,' one of the visitors wrote afterwards, 'before we could summon enough courage to ask for the book back, to return it to the minister.' The old man needed no stars: they were in his eyes: but I hope he got one – and soon after, a Bible of his own.

Providing good books, including the Bible, is as important as teaching people to read. That means hard work translating and printing things worth reading. One teacher was having trouble finding a word in the language of his African tribe to translate the Bible word 'redeem' – which means to buy back into freedom. He consulted his African Christian friends, and they talked it over among themselves. Then one suggested 'Kounmabo'. 'But why,' said the teacher, 'for surely *kounmabo* means "take out the head".'

'Exactly,' said the Africans, 'that's just it. You see, when in the old days slave raiders captured men and took them down to the coast in chains and iron collars, it sometimes happened that a chief or other leading man would learn that a friend, or a friend's son, had been caught. He would go and bargain for the captive, and pay money: and if he paid enough, the collar on that boy would be unlocked, his head taken out, and he would go free – for a price.' So into the translation the African word went: By his death for us upon the cross, Jesus 'took our heads out' and set us free.

In the Eskimo translation (remember all those lovely husky dogs, racing over the ice pulling sledges!), it was hard to find a word for 'glad'. The Eskimos seem a very solemn, even a sad-looking, people. In the end, the Psalmist is made to say, in Eskimo language, 'I wagged my tail when they said unto me, Let us go into the igloo of God.'

One small African boy had a hard time in boarding school, having to learn a new language for all his lessons, and even in church. One day, someone gave him a Gospel in his own home-language, and at once he felt the difference it made. He felt now that God was speaking directly to him. 'Please may I take this home with me,' he asked very eagerly; 'I want to read it to my parents and to all my friends. For these words make holes in my heart!'

How do *you* read?

49 Courageous Praise

It is easy, when we remember, to praise God for all that we enjoy, for plans that work out well, for things that go right, for holidays and friends, and birthdays, and success, and gifts and all the rest. It takes a great deal of courage to go on trusting God, and thanking him, when what you want very much does not come, when plans go wrong, and all your hard work brings no success. We *can* thank God, even then, for he is still good, and his love does not change. It is just that he knows best what is good for us. But to say 'Yes, Lord. Let it be just as *you* say. I still praise you, and thank you' demands a brave heart.

A writer of fine short stories, named E Tegla Davies, tells of a poor Welsh farmer, Samuel Jones, who one year found himself out of tune with his wealthier neighbours at harvest-festival time. They were making great plans to decorate their little chapel with a proud display of corn and berries, fruit and vegetable, to say 'Thank you' to God for another successful year of farming. He had only very poor grain, and small crops, wrested by hard work from sun-starved land on the shadowed side of the hill. There the weeds grew strongest, and the cold winter rains lasted longest, and the soil was thin and poor. It was not his fault, but try as he might, he could not get the crops his neighbours got.

That year, things had been worse than ever, and as harvest-festival came round, he felt right out of it. Instead of turning up on Saturday to help get the chapel ready, he went off for a long, unhappy walk by himself, thinking over things with a bitter, envious heart. In the end, he resolved not to go the chapel on the Sunday: he had no worship in his heart.

He lay awake a long time that night. In the end he got up, and tried to pray: and that made him remember happier days, and things he used to enjoy so much, and how good his life had been in other ways. He thought too how well he had always been, able to struggle year after year with his hard soil without illness; and how there had always been enough, though not as much as he would have liked. He thought too of Christ, and how much he owed to him, for forgiveness of many things done wrong, and for help and salvation. As the morning came, he felt better, almost joyous. Certainly he saw things more clearly. Then he had an idea.

He went down to the chapel early, long before anyone else would come. And he took with him some of his poor grain, and nettles, and thistles and dock-leaves and brambles as well. Very carefully, he removed all the lovely things his neighbours had placed in chapel, taking them to a back room for later on. And in their place he decorated the chapel with his own things – not at all a bright display, with the drooping, dark-stained wheat, the dull dock-leaves, and the sorry-looking brambles and weeds. Then he waited.

As the congregation began to arrive, they found him there, quietly praying. They were struck dumb, and took their places very, very thoughtfully. They were not angry, for they knew Samuel Jones to be a godly man; he often conducted the service for them, and they liked to have him preach. So they knew he must mean something, but they did not really understand. The singing, when service began, was poor, very poor for a *Welsh* harvest-festival; and the prayers were very quiet, too. How could men see God's goodness in thistles, weeds, brambles and gorse. Men and women who had long worshipped God for his bounty, found it hard to praise him surrounded by all the signs of toil and failure, and poor harvest.

Then Samuel Jones stepped into the pulpit, and with a new light in his eyes, he began to read from that little book by an ancient prophet whose name no one can spell – the prophet Habakkuk (I looked it up):

'Though the fig trees do not blossom,
    nor fruit be on the vines,
the produce of the olive fail
    and the fields yield no food,
the flock be cut off from the fold
    and there be no herd in the stalls,
yet I will rejoice in the Lord,
    I will joy in the God of my salvation.'

Quietly, Samuel Jones reminded the congregation that figs and vines, olives and crops, provided the work and wealth of the Israelites, so that what Habakkuk was saying amounted to: 'though the factories stand idle and the mines are deserted, though gardens and fields are barren and the shops are empty, though business fails, work ceases, and health and home are taken from us, *yet* will we rejoice in the Lord; though nothing goes right, and my heart is disappointed after all my labour, yet I will praise God, for all his goodness and loving-kindness, for he has never yet failed me, or forsaken me, nor ceased to love.'

Then Samuel Jones led the congregation in a prayer that was long remembered, thanking God amid the nettles and the brambles, not simply for what he gives, but for all that he is to us, when things are hard.

It takes a brave heart to praise like that.

50 Two Sorts of Ships

Long, long ago, Jehoshaphat king of Israel made him 'ships of Tarshish to go to Ophir for gold: but they went not, for they were broken at Ezion Geber'.

That short, sad story needs a little explaining. The Jews generally did not like the sea, unlike the Greeks, who loved it, as most island peoples, or peoples with a long coastline, do. Yet the Jews had some good sailors.

Solomon the king, in the days of his greatness built himself a large navy, and as his power grew so he dreamed of the treasures in many lands which he could discover, or plunder, or extort by taxes. So he built more ships, sailing ships of course, at the mercy of every wind, but big, strong, sea-worthy ships, able to do a three-year voyage on stormy seas to far distant places like Tarshish. They were massive vessels, known in fact as Tarshish-ships, from their size and strength, and ability to stay at sea for so long. And Solomon grew immensely rich.

But Jehoshaphat was neither great, nor wise, nor powerful like Solomon; he copied Solomon only in his dreaming. He too thought of all that distant wealth and treasure, and built his Tarshish-ships. He intended them to go to Ophir, which many people think was way down the eastern coast of Africa on the Indian Ocean. And Jehoshaphat moored his ships in the deep water near the Red Sea, at the end of the long deep valley through which the Jordan flows, and south of where the Dead Sea lies. There they waited, sheltered, but idle.

What they waited *for*, we do not know: for men courageous enough to man them? for weather calm enough to sail? or for the king, who was rather a weak man, to make up his mind to risk his fine ships on the open sea?

Anyhow, while they waited, a strong wind started up in that long, narrow river-valley, usually so sheltered. As it rushed down the channel between high rocky cliffs and over the Dead Sea, it became a gale; the gale became a hurricane, and before anything could be done, all the fine ships were smashed *in port*, at their anchorage. Tangled sails and broken masts, smashed decks and stove-in sides, were all that was left of proud and costly ships that never saw the sea.

Not so long ago, towards the end of the days of sailing ships, a fine three-masted barque called *'The Wanderer'* was built at Liverpool, in northern England. She too was strong, and proud, but just as soon as she was ship-shape and ready, she set sail into the Irish sea in wild weather. No waiting for brave sailors or safe seas, in her case. Only a few miles beyond the shelter of land, the wild weather became a mighty storm, and the fine new ship suffered badly. It was no one's fault: weather forecasting was almost unknown in those days, and radio-warnings undreamed-of. *'The Wanderer'* could only ride out the storm; her top sails were blown away, her main-mast snapped; some of the crew were badly wounded; and trying to save one man, her Captain, a fine man named George Currie, was killed by a falling spar.

'The Wanderer' had to turn back, crippled, from her maiden voyage, and limp into Liverpool again, her flag at half-mast, her sails torn, her crew weary, grieving and down-hearted. The wounded were carried away to hospital. The rest of the men watched over their dead Captain. Then the battered ship was towed away for repair.

She sailed again, but somehow she was unfortunate. She met one storm after another, saw one disaster after another, and in the end, with the reputation of 'a tragic ship', she was broken up before her time. But at least she sailed. As sailors say, 'she met her storms upon the open sea', not sheltering – skulking – in port.

Here are two kinds of ships, both battered and destroyed. And there are two kinds of people. Some men, women, young people, are all fitted out with fine chances and great promise, a good education, real gifts of personality, clever brains, and much to encourage them: but they get nowhere, achieve noth-ing worthwhile. They are 'full of promise' and of nothing else. Somehow they lack the will to work, or the faith to try, or the courage to act: they continue to depend on other people, shel-

tering in safe places, doing no good and bringing home no car-
goes, because they *do* nothing.

While some other people (not all), with far less gifts of education, personality, opportunity, but with large hearts, and
great faith, and high courage, and the will to do splendid
things for others and for God, achieve surprisingly great
things. Most of the great people of the world had good
excuses not to be great, but they tried. They set sail, they
faced the storms: they were battered, but in the end they
brought home treasure, in fine character and good things
accomplished.

A young Welsh lad, with little money and no great gifts,
planned to open a shop – a tiny place at the corner of two
mean streets. His name was Billy Cant: but he would not paint
that up, he made it Billy Cann. Before long he had a second
shop, and because he knew what people were saying about
him, he painted over that one, 'Who'd Have Thought?'
People knew what he was selling, and the name made him
talked about more than any advertisement. So soon he had a
third shop, and this time, after much thought, he painted over
it 'Well, I Never!'

I like that. At any rate he got out of Ezion Geber, without
very much on board, and deserved to come home laden with
good things.

51 Carried by Four

The *first* man was Gamaliel, a famous Rabbi (teacher) in Jerusalem at about the time of Jesus. He was wise, his students honoured him, and many consulted him about their problems and their doubts.

Among his students was a specially bright young man from distant Tarsus, who outstripped all his rivals of the same age in his speed of learning and his depth of understanding. That student's name was Saul, and everyone thought that one day he would take his master's place as the most important teacher of the Jews.

Gamaliel taught, of course, the Jewish religion, the stories of the Old Testament, and the wonderful promises of God to Israel. He also taught to young Saul a profound faith in God. For the chief thing we know about Gamaliel is that once, when the Christian church was just beginning in Jerusalem, and Peter and John had been arrested and brought before the Jewish council to answer for teaching and healing in Jesus' name, Gamaliel gave the council some very wise advice. 'Take care what you do with these men,' he said, 'let them alone. For if their plan and undertaking is of men, it will fail. If it is of God, you will not be able to overthrow them, you might even be found to be opposing God!'

That is good sense. It is no use trying to fight against God. You are bound to be in the wrong, and bound to lose, as well. God always gets his way in time. Young Saul must have heard Gamaliel speak like that many times, for he never forgot the lesson.

The *second* man was Stephen. He was a fine young Christian in Jerusalem, appointed at first to help distribute the gifts of Christians among the poor. But Stephen also preached the gospel, and with such eloquence and power that a great stir was raised in Jerusalem by his boldness and skill. Many were persuaded to become Christians. Many others

186

187

were made very angry at his success, and because they could not answer his arguments, their anger turned to violence, and they began to throw stones. Stephen did not run away; he stayed, and preached, until one stone knocked him over. Falling to his knees, he prayed for those who were attacking him, and so he died.

It was a tragic end to a promising young life, and a dreadful blow to the other Christians. But among the crowd who watched, and minding the clothes of the stone-throwers, urging them on, was the same brilliant young student, Saul of Tarsus. Afterwards, Saul was very troubled about what had happened. The character of Stephen, his preaching, and above all his prayer of forgiveness, not bitterness, remained in Saul's memory all his life, as his later letters show. It nagged his conscience that he had helped to kill young Stephen; he believed later that God had forgiven him for it, but he found it hard to forgive himself.

The *third* man was Ananias. He was a leading Christian at Damascus, some miles north of Jerusalem, and he comes into Saul's story in a strange way. At first, Saul had tried to silence his troubled conscience by persecuting Christians all the more; for that purpose he rode off to Damascus, where he had been told there was a Christian church, to try to stamp it out. But (as I am sure you know) just outside Damascus something totally unexpected happened. He received 'a heavenly vision': the risen Lord Jesus appeared to him, spoke to him, changed him, leaving him blinded and confused. Among other things, Jesus told Saul to send into Damascus for Ananias, and learn from him what to do next.

About the same time, Jesus appeared also to Ananias, telling him to seek out Saul and teach him the Christian way. But Ananias objected that Saul was a persecutor, and to go to him was dangerous. In the end he went, however, hailed Saul as his 'brother', healed his blindness, and baptised him into the fellowship of the Christian church. Probably it was at his baptism, that the young student's name was changed, from the rather proud, royal name of 'Saul' to the much humbler one, 'Paul', which means *little*.

The *fourth* man in Paul's story is Barnabas – 'a good man, full of the Holy Spirit, and of faith'. He was a splendid friend to Paul. When Paul went up to Jerusalem, to meet his new Christian friends, he found them very suspicious and afraid. They still thought of him as an enemy, only pretending to be a Christian in order to learn their meeting places, and who were Christians in Jerusalem. But Barnabas went out to speak to him, to listen to his story of meeting with Jesus, and to hear his confession of faith in Christ. Then Barnabas brought him in to where the Christian leaders were, and assured them that Paul really was a Christian. Barnabas made himself a sort of guarantor for Paul's sincerity: that satisfied the church, and they welcomed Paul gladly.

A little later, at another city called Antioch, a new church needed a leader and teacher to guide them in God's work. Barnabas had been sent there by the other leaders in Jerusalem, and he could have taken charge himself. Instead, he went off to Tarsus, where Paul had gone to think out his new faith, and what to do with his life now that all was changed for him; and Barnabas brought him back to Antioch, to be leader and pastor of the new church. What is more, he stayed there himself beside young Paul, to encourage, advise, and uphold him. So Paul got his first chance in the work of God, that was presently to make him the greatest of all the apostles. And he owed that opportunity, as he owed his welcome into the church, to the trust, and friendship, and selflessness, of Barnabas.

In the Gospels we read of a paralyzed man who was carried to Jesus by four friends, and let down on his bed through the roof into the house where Jesus was. It seems true that the great Paul, also, was carried to Jesus by four friends –

by Gamaliel, who never intended him to be a Christian, but taught him not to fight against God:

by Stephen, who never even knew that he had helped;

by Ananias, who had been so reluctant to help;

by Barnabas, who came late but helped greatly.

So,

God uses us to help each other so,
Lending our minds out . . .

It is good that we should never forget who taught *us* the love of Jesus, and how many have helped us along the Christian way.

52 Caught You!

This story is not quite what it seems: read carefully!

Think of a great wide lake, of smooth, still water under an evening sky. The almost motionless surface catches the clear light on its tiny ripples, and reflects the ring of green hills that surrounds the lake. Small boats are lazily moving to and fro, or bobbing idly at the water's edge; and in the quiet evening air every sound seems to be magnified as it is carried clearly across the water.

In the prow of one boat, a young man is talking to those nearest to him, but his voice carries to others. He is speaking, evidently of God, and what God means to him: and he seems to be appealing to the others to seek and to find God's kingdom, to discover what is the will of God for their own lives.

In one of the other boats is another young man, listening intently. Already he has almost decided to follow Jesus, and to devote his life to the work of God's kingdom – but not quite. Now, as he listens, his heart is thrilled. He feels impelled towards decision, and sitting there within the boat on the quiet water on a still evening, he makes the momentous resolve that will change his whole life. 'O God,' he prayed, 'you know that I do not want anything but to serve you and men, always, all my life.' That night he wrote in his diary, 'These words and thoughts will, I hope, be with me all my life.'

Soon he determined to be a missionary, and he meant to be the very best that he could be for Christ. So, instead of rushing off impetuously to some distant place to throw himself into Christian work with enthusiasm but no skill, he first went up to University to train. Then, during training, he sought out what seemed to him to be the hardest work requiring to be done; what was the most difficult place in which to preach the gospel; who were likely to be the most unresponsive people; and what is their language, easy to learn, or hard.

All four questions had the same answer: the hardest work,

to preach Christ among Mohammedans, the most difficult place, Egypt; the most unresponsive people, probably the Arabs; and the hardest language – almost indistinguishable squiggles on paper, and a rattle of harsh sounds in speech – Arabic. So off he went.

For the young man listening in the boat was Temple Gairdner; the hills were not of Palestine, but of northern England, and the lake not Galilee but Derwentwater. The speaker was an unknown Christian of our century.

Gairdner fulfilled his promises with enormous energy. He mastered the several strange languages of Egypt until he could speak almost like a native. He studied Mohammedan teaching and philosophy as though he was training to become a Mohammedan leader! Disguised as an Arab, he lived for weeks among the bazaars and mosques of Aleppo, until he could not only look and sound, but think and feel like a Mohammedan. He did everything he could to understand, and sympathise, and to draw close to the people he wanted to serve in Christ's name.

To help others to do the same, Gairdner opened a school of Egyptian languages in the great city of Cairo, and with it a Christian bookshop. He established a two-language newspaper, to give Christian news, comment, and explanation. To make Christian faith and worship easier to understand for the Egyptian people, he collected the hymns of the ancient Egyptian church, the songs of boatmen on the Nile, the chants used by Egypt's own holy men, and from them all he produced an Egyptian Christian hymnbook.

When the first great war began, Gairdner stayed on in Cairo to help young soldiers, sailors, and airmen, the wounded and the prisoners. Yet another experiment of this tireless man was the writing of Christian plays in Arabic, to teach Arabs the gospel by looking, as well as by listening and reading. When he died, at fifty-five years of age, Gairdner 'left in Egypt the imperishable memory of one who, more than most, had drawn the Arab world nearer to Christ'.

Gairdner's is a fine story: but remember how and where it all began, listening to the voice coming across the water of the lake, inviting others to follow and serve the kingdom of God. Then remember this:

'And passing along by the Sea of Galilee, Jesus saw Simon and Andrew the brother of Simon casting a net in the sea; for they were fishermen. And Jesus said to them, "Follow me and I will make you become fishers of men." And immediately they left their nets and followed him. And going on a little farther, he saw James the son of Zebedee and John his brother, who were in their boat mending the nets. And immediately he called them; and they left their father Zebedee in the boat with the hired servants, and followed him.'

It is truly wonderful how incidents in the gospel story keep being repeated down the years, as the living Jesus still calls, and sends, his own men and women into his service.

Truly wonderful, too, to respond so whole-heartedly, so devotedly, as Temple Gairdner did.